Asserting
Your Self

Asserting Your Self

*How to feel confident about
getting more from life*

CATHY BIRCH

How To Books

Published by How To Books Ltd, 3 Newtec Place,
Magdalen Road, Oxford OX4 1RE, United Kingdom
Tel: (01865) 793806   Fax: (01865) 248780
email: info@howtobooks.co.uk
www.howtobooks.co.uk

First edition 1999
Reprinted 2000

British Library Cataloguing in Publication Data
A catalogue record for this book is available from
the British Library

Editing by Diana Brueton
Cover design by Shireen Nathoo Design
Cover image PhotoDisc

Produced for How To Books by Deer Park Productions
Typeset by Concept Communications Ltd, Crayford, Kent
Printed and bound by Cromwell Press, Trowbridge, Wiltshire

NOTE: The material contained in this book is set out in good
faith for general guidance and no liability can be accepted
for loss or expense incurred as a result of relying in particular
circumstances on statements made in the book. The laws and
regulations are complex and liable to change, and readers should
check the current position with the relevant authorities before
making personal arrangements.

Contents

List of illustrations

Preface

What gifts did the good fairies bestow on Sleeping Beauty at her christening? In various versions of the story we see listed such attributes as beauty, intelligence, grace, kindness, musical skills – but never assertiveness. How interesting that this all important gift should be overlooked, when its effects would have rendered the fairies themselves redundant and halted the ensuing mayhem before it began.

An assertive person does not need to wait passively for the granting of favours. An assertive daughter might have told her father, 'I really appreciate your concern, but I feel this total ban on needles is an over-reaction.' She would not have been fooled by the old woman in the tower. She would not have required a hedge of thorns to protect her, nor a prince (who certainly took his time) to come and rescue her. In fact, she would probably have pre-empted the entire sequence of events by disarming the thirteenth fairy's fury at the start. With the gift of assertiveness firmly on board she might have sat up in her cradle and said, 'I can see you are very angry, and you have good reason to be. Let's go somewhere quiet where we can talk about this.'

A healthily assertive attitude puts us in charge of our own destiny – which can be somewhat upsetting to anyone who would like to control it for us. As members of society we are, on the whole, conditioned not to prize such an attitude other than as an attribute of 'those in charge'. Not surprisingly, it is seldom taught in schools.

This book aims to redress that balance by showing you how to replace unproductive attitudes and behaviours, with a way of being which will enrich every aspect of your life.

Cathy Birch

1

Looking at Assertiveness

Northumberland has been described in its tourist literature as 'Britain's best kept secret', suggesting that if too many people found out about it, this would spoil things for those already 'in the know'. A similar observation might be made about assertiveness. What would happen if large numbers of people began to acquire these skills? Would the world be full of brash egotistical extraverts all demanding their own way?

Some people are uncomfortable with the idea of assertiveness because they associate it with being pushy, 'hard' or otherwise unapproachable. What do you feel about this?

DEFINING YOUR TERMS

What does the word 'assertiveness' mean to you? Jot down any phrases or images which come to mind when you hear that word.

Here are some definitions elicited from workshop participants over the years. Assertiveness means:

- Being able to ask clearly for what I want or need.

- Having the confidence to say what I am feeling.

- Having clear personal boundaries and being able to state them.

- Feeling comfortable about saying 'I' – not 'we', 'you' or 'one'.

- Recognising that I have wants and needs, and doing something about them.

- Feeling comfortable about asking for help.

- Taking responsibility for my thoughts, feelings and actions.

- Not feeling responsible for other people's thoughts, feelings and actions.

- Saying 'I choose to' rather than 'I have to'.

- Having the confidence to make mistakes and admit them.

- Feeling comfortable with success.

- Being able to stand up to aggressive people.

- Being able to state the adverse affect someone's behaviour is having on me.

- Being able to say 'no' and stick to it.

- Being able to say 'no' without feelings of guilt.

- Feeling comfortable with criticism or praise – able to view both objectively.

- Being able to speak out when appropriate.

- Having the confidence to remain silent when appropriate.

- Being able to deal with a situation confidently, and in a manner which takes due account of the other person's viewpoint and feelings.

Understanding assertiveness

People who feel wary of assertiveness may be confusing it with **aggression** – a defensive reaction whereby we try to overcome feelings of fear or inadequacy by 'looking big'. Assertiveness is not like this. It is strongly associated with a sense of **self-worth**. When we truly value ourselves we have no need to use **power games** or manipulative behaviour to get what we want – nor are we at the mercy of those who try to use these ploys to influence us. We can relate to others honestly, stating our needs clearly and respecting theirs while not feeling compelled to fulfil them.

CONSIDERING THE BENEFITS

Developing a healthily assertive attitude can transform every aspect of our lives: our work, our relationships, our appearance, the way we shop, the way we feed and clothe ourselves, the way we organise our finances, the way we spend our leisure time – indeed, taking time out for leisure in the first place is an assertive act. Being able to express feelings constructively and be open with others – and ourselves – about our needs, maximises our chances of getting what we want in all these areas. This in turn increases our confidence and our self-esteem, which enables us to become more assertive and so on. Figure 1, the assertiveness cycle, illustrates this cumulative effect; a case of success breeds success.

Living assertively can also benefit our health. Reduction of stress levels makes more energy available to us and has a beneficial effect on all systems of the body, including the immune system. From another viewpoint, writers such as Louise Hay and Thorwald Dethlefsen (see Further Reading) would say that clear personal boundaries and a sense of self-worth help to protect us from invasion by other organisms – including germs.

CHECKLIST

Assertiveness:

- is very different from aggression

- is strongly associated with a sense of self-worth

- can benefit every aspect of our lives, including our health.

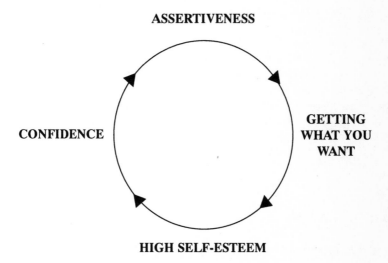

Fig. 1. The assertiveness cycle.

ASSESSING YOUR NEEDS

Finding out where you are

Use the assertiveness self-assessment (Figure 2) to find your present assertiveness levels, and to help pinpoint areas which might need some work. (Keep your scores for reference at a later date.) Of course there are situations when it is appropriate to keep a low profile by behaving non-assertively. However, should non-assertiveness become a habit rather than a considered choice, we may frequently feel at a disadvantage. The rest of this chapter and the chapters which follow suggest some ways of changing this.

Noticing what you do

Look at the list of non-verbal behaviour signals (Figure 3) and note any which apply to you (a friend's feedback would be helpful). Which type of behaviour do you tend to exhibit most – passive, aggressive, manipulative or assertive? If you found that a number of behaviours in the first three sections applied to you, some changes may need to be made. Awareness of what you are doing is, of course, the first step in this process. As we begin to catch ourselves in the act and make the changes we want, we start to look and sound more confident. People then begin to react to us in a different way and our confidence increases.

USING A ROLE MODEL

Who do you know who is really assertive? Use the self-assessment statements and the definitions given in this chapter to help you choose a person who would make a good **role model**. What do they do and say which makes you see them as assertive? Find an opportunity to watch them carefully. Observe their body language and their speech habits, just as though you were an actor studying a role. Take particular note of:

● posture

● when they move and when they are still

● how they move

● their tone of voice, manner of speaking and the words they use

● facial expression – particularly their eyebrows (see Further Tips below).

Check your observations against the list of non-verbal behaviour signals in Figure 3. When you have made a thorough study, imagine you are that assertive person. Practise moving like them and speaking like them until it feels easy. When you need to be assertive, think what that person would do and say. Copy them until you feel confident enough to do it your own way.

Further tips

1. Eyebrow control is crucial in the early stages of becoming assertive. (As you become more proficient, your eyebrows will take care of themselves!) Raised eyebrows can signal lack of assurance or a wish to please. Pulled down eyebrows can signal aggression or puzzlement. The assertive eyebrow position is relaxed, and keeping your eyebrows in this state can greatly enhance your effectiveness.

2. Opening phrases are very important. Do not apologise unless an apology is called for. Do not make excuses, marginalise yourself or put yourself down. If you open with 'I'm sorry to be a nuisance', or 'I'm sorry to bother you', you are asking to be seen as a nuisance and bothersome.

3. Avoid qualifiers such as 'just', 'only' and 'sort of'. They dampen the impact of your message.

4. Establish good eye contact with the person you are talking to. Make sure you have their full attention.

5. Never try to make yourself small – either physically by hunching yourself up, or verbally by speaking in a small or high-pitched voice. This immediately hands power to the person you are addressing.

CHECKLIST

Behaviour change:

● begins with self-awareness

● requires a clear picture of what we want to achieve

● can cause others to react in ways which make us feel more confident

● can be helped by having good role models.

How well do these statements describe you?
Mark yourself on a scale of 0–10 for each one.

I can deal with most situations confidently, while respecting
others' viewpoints and feelings.   _____

I feel comfortable when other people behave assertively.   _____

I have the confidence to state positively what I want,
need and feel.   _____

I have the confidence to ask for time to think things over.   _____

I recognise my own wants and needs as separate from
those of others.   _____

I have clear personal boundaries and can state them.   _____

I respect myself, who I am and what I do.   _____

I take responsibility for myself, my thoughts, my actions
and my feelings.   _____

I am responsible *towards* others – not *for* them
(unless they are children).   _____

I allow myself to make mistakes and have the confidence
to admit them.   _____

I allow myself to enjoy my successes.   _____

I can stand up to aggressive people.   _____

I make clear 'I' statements about my thoughts and feelings.   _____

I can state the adverse affect somebody's behaviour is
having on me.   _____

I can say 'no' and stick to it.   _____

I can say 'no' without feelings of guilt.   _____

I say 'I choose to' rather than 'I have to'.   _____

I allow myself to change my mind.   _____

I feel comfortable with criticism or praise. I am able to
view both objectively.   _____

I have the confidence to speak out when appropriate.   _____

I have the confidence to remain silent when appropriate.   _____

Fig. 2. Assertiveness self-assessment.

	Use of voice	Facial expression	Body language
Aggressive	Domineering Sarcastic Cold Hard-edged Strident, loud Menacingly quiet Deliberate Little or no hesitation Often brusque, clipped Often fast Stress on blaming words	Wry or sarcastic smile Scowl Jaw set Teeth clenched Chin jutting Gaze held too long Eyes narrowed Staring over the top of glasses Eyebrows raised mockingly One eyebrow raised	Finger pointing Fist thumping Rigid back/ shoulders Leaning forward Coming too close Striding about Angry foot/ finger tapping Folding arms impatiently Hands on hips Turning away abruptly
Passive	Shaky Sing-song Whining Too soft Placating tone Dull/monotone Swallowing words Hesitant/jerky Throat clearing Stress on self-effacing words	Fixed smile Smiling when angry or sad Smiling to pacify Facial tic Fast changing expression Avoiding eye-contact Eyebrows raised anxiously	Wringing hands Fiddling/ fidgeting Stepping back Leaning away Hunching shoulders Covering mouth Shrugging Shuffling feet Tapping foot anxiously Hugging self
Manipulative	Too smooth Too warm Dramatic pauses Hypnotic inflection Over-enthusiastic Ingratiating Sympathy seeking Sighing Dropping voice deliberately Chuckling conspiratorially Stress on persuasive words	Ingratiating smile Sad smile Calculating Assumed for effect – not real Eyes darting Eyebrows often raised	Conspiratorial closeness Intrusive touching Dramatic gestures
Assertive	Steady, firm Medium pitch Medium volume Sincere Appropriate warmth Clear Fluent Steady pace Stress on key words	Smiles appropriately Frowns appropriately Open expression Features steady Jaw relaxed Holds gaze calmly Eyebrows level	Open gestures Upright relaxed gestures Head held straight Hands/limbs at rest

Fig. 3. Non-verbal behaviour signals.

SKILLS PRACTICE

Making an entrance

Use your observations plus the further tips listed above to help you with this exercise, which is based on a real incident.

It was lunch time in the offices of a big company, so very few staff were present. There was a timid scratching at the door and a sales rep sidled in clutching a briefcase to his chest with both arms. Eyes downcast, eyebrows raised, he mumbled 'I don't suppose anyone wants to buy some encyclopaedias.' His supposition at least was spot on!

1. If you were his manager, what would you advise him to say and do in future to improve his performance?

2. In role as the sales rep, make an entrance. Deliver your message in the new and assertive manner.

KEEPING A PROGRESS JOURNAL

As with any self-development programme, the benefits of working with this book will be greatly enhanced by keeping a daily journal of your progress. Record everything – your successes and the things which went less well. Analyse the reasons for these outcomes. Think of things you might do differently next time. Write something each day while it is fresh in your mind, even if you only have time for a few comments.

As well as indicating where work might be needed, a journal also shows the progress you have made over a long period. If you sometimes have the feeling that you are getting nowhere, it can be very encouraging to look back and see that changes have indeed taken place since the start of the programme.

Persevering

Becoming assertive requires determination and persistence. Like any skill, it requires practice and more practice and the ability not to be disheartened if you get it wrong. A useful way not to beat yourself up on such occasions is to say 'I wasn't very effective that time' rather than 'I am not very good at this'. You can then put it aside as being just *one incident* and move on.

CASE STUDIES

Howard wants his wife to mind-read

Howard is in his early 50s. From age 9 he was educated in a boarding school where 'emotional displays' were discouraged. His parents did not understand his distress at being separated from them and wanted him to 'be sensible'. Hiding his feelings and surviving without emotional support from those he loved became a way of life. In his work as a biochemist he has little contact with others. In his 30s he married Jenny, a woman 12 years his junior whom he could 'look after'. Now that she is in her late 30s and becoming increasingly independent, this no longer works. Jenny is upset that Howard does not share his feelings with her. Howard is hurt that Jenny does not know how he feels without being told, but he is unable to say so.

Everyone depends on Stella

Stella is 45. As the youngest of three daughters, she has spent years caring for her elderly parents and had resigned herself to this role. Other elderly relatives also rely on her to run errands and give them lifts, as do a number of friends and neighbours who look on her as a 'good sort'. She has assumed a similar role in her marriage so that her husband Jeff and two teenaged sons have become used to being waited on. She feels unable to say no to anybody's requests. Since her mother's death a year ago, her father has become very demanding and critical. She finds this upsetting, but is unable to confront him. Stella is feeling increasingly stressed and wonders how much longer she can continue to be there for so many people.

Andrew has learned to be hard

Andrew, 32, is Howard's neighbour. He comes from a large family and grew up in a tough neighbourhood where he learned to be street-wise at an early age. In his teens he won a number of amateur boxing trophies, and he helps to run the local boxing club in his spare time. He also plays rugby. Andrew runs his own double-glazing business, which is doing well. He thinks Howard is soft, but he takes advantage of his neighbour's good nature when it suits him. Andrew's aggressive attitude often alienates him from people. In the past he dismissed this as 'the name of the game'. However, his wife Sandra has recently admitted that she and their two young children are afraid of his temper. This has shocked him into wanting to change his behaviour.

GETTING THE MOST FROM THIS CHAPTER

1. Observe your own behaviour closely and ask for a friend's feedback.

2. Spend some time choosing a good role model and observe them carefully.

3. Practise your skills frequently.

4. Start a journal and make sure you record your progress every day.

5. Persevere.

2

Dealing with the Past

Look again at the self-assessment statements in Chapter 1. Which ones did you feel applied to you least? Could this be a family thing? In your family of origin, was assertiveness in those areas actively discouraged? Did you inherit your attitude from a non-assertive family member? What about school? Did you develop a set of non-assertive responses to that environment in order to survive? If so, have they stuck? If not, what other events in your life might have caused you to feel unconfident about making the statements in question?

Identifying the original sources of our non-assertive feelings and behaviours can be extremely helpful. Some will turn out to be other people's baggage which we did not realise we were carrying. Some may reveal themselves as defences against old hurts. Others will be recognised as survival mechanisms which were needed to get us through a difficult period in our lives. Most will prove to be old programs which no longer serve us and which we need to discard or to change in some way.

Our most powerful programming is likely to have occurred within our family of origin.

REPLAYING THE FAMILY DRAMAS

Assembling the characters

Take a few moments to bring to mind the members of your family who influenced you most. Think about them in relation to the statements you found difficult. For example:

- Who might have disapproved of those particular statements?

- Who did not allow mistakes?

- Who might have been uncomfortable with self-promotion?

- Who might have felt threatened by assertive behaviour?

- Who found it hard to say 'no'?

- Who was afraid of success?

How might these non-assertive attitudes have affected you?

The physical and vocal mannerisms of certain family members may also have been unconsciously copied and carried over into your adult life. Just as good role models can teach us more productive ways of behaving, less helpful models can have the opposite effect.

Look again at the list of non-verbal behaviour signals in Figure 3. Do you recognise any of them as applying to you? A friend's feedback would be helpful here. Who might you be imitating when you behave in these ways? What might have led you to imitate their behaviour in the past? What reasons might you have for continuing to do this as an adult?

Of the four main types of behaviour listed, which is most characteristic of you? Are you happy with this? If not, what changes would you like to make?

CHECKLIST

Non-assertive behaviour, both verbal and non-verbal:

● may have been copied

● may have defended you from being hurt

● may have helped you to survive a difficult time

● may have been encouraged in your family of origin

● is something you have learned to do

● is something which you can change.

REWRITING THE SCRIPT

A very useful step in working towards behaviour change can be the identification of original role-models and the use of the imagination to interact with them.

In the two taped exercises which follow you can try this approach for yourself, working with one self-assessment statement and one behaviour you would like to change. In these and other taped exercises throughout this book, we will be using various combinations of the following psychotherapeutic techniques:

- visualisation

- dramatisation

- thinking of a title

- finding an image

- inventing and naming a character with the trait in question

- exaggerating behaviour

- working with opposites

- affirming the changes.

These techniques are useful in any situation where we wish to explore words, images, gestures and feelings more fully. The questions and instructions for the exercises should be read onto a tape, leaving suitable pauses for your response.

Exercise 1: Working with a statement

- Choose one of the self-assessment statements that caused you some difficulty.

- Rewrite the beginning as 'It is not right/not safe to . . .'. Which member of your family might have said that?

- Picture them saying it. Notice their expression, their body language, their voice.

- Become that person now. Move like them. Make the negative statement in their voice. How does this feel?

- Why does this person feel that way? What would it take to change those feelings? Imagine that change taking place.

- What would it take to change your feelings? Imagine that change taking place.

- First as the person in question then as yourself, make the original 'I' statement, adding 'and that feels *good*.' Repeat this until you feel confident in saying it.

● Repeat the process with other statements you found difficult.

Exercise 2: Working with a non-verbal behaviour

● Choose a non-verbal behaviour you would like to change. Who else in your family behaves like this? (If nobody comes to mind, continue the exercise as yourself.)

● Become that person. Act out the behaviour you have chosen. Exaggerate it – make it bigger/louder/faster. How does that feel?

● What would the opposite of that behaviour be? Act out that opposite behaviour now. Exaggerate it. How does that feel?

● Experiment with these different behaviours for a while. Switch between them.

● Find an appropriate nickname for somebody who behaves the first way and another nickname for somebody who behaves the opposite way.

● What do you like about each of these people? What do you dislike?

● Which aspects of their behaviour will you keep? Which will you discard?

● Repeat the exercise with other non-verbal behaviours you would like to change.

REWRITING THE FAMILY HISTORY

Of course it is not only isolated incidents and people, but whole areas of our family history which affect the way we feel about ourselves. Our family members are like a cast of characters which we carry round inside us, each playing out their own particular scenes in our personal drama.

Some of the people and events concerned have had a positive effect on our lives. Others have been upsetting, disruptive and in some cases may have changed the family fortunes drastically. Together they make up the family history which is stored in the vault of our subconscious and which surfaces in the stories we tell ourselves as we try to make sense of our lives. 'I blame it all on . . .' 'I owe it all to . . .' 'If only . . .'. Once we understand this process, we can begin to use it in a positive way.

Exercise 3: Experiencing the positive and negative energies of your family history

● Call to mind some of the significant events in your family saga. Notice your feelings as you think about them. What happens to your energy as you switch your attention from a happy event to one which caused the family some misfortune?

● Choose one event which had a positive impact on your life. Picture it in great detail. What was so good about it? How do you feel as you think about it?

● Who were the main family members involved? Think about each in turn. What role did they play? How do you feel towards them as you think about that event?

● What enabled that positive event to come about? What resulted from it? What influence might it have on your life now?

● Choose one event which had a negative impact on your life. Picture it in great detail. What was so bad about it? How do you feel as you remember it?

● Who were the main family members involved? Take some time to think about each one in turn. What role did they play? Would it have been possible for them to act differently in that situation?

● How do you feel towards them as you think about that event?

● What influence might this event have on your life now?

● What would you have done in their place?

You probably felt quite elated and encouraged as you recalled the positive events. You may have experienced positive feelings towards those involved. Recalling the negative events probably felt quite different. Whatever your feelings towards the family members concerned, you may also have felt anger, regret, resentment, maybe guilt, about the event itself.

Feelings about the past can strongly colour the way we see ourselves. Good feelings boost our self-esteem. Negative ones bring us down, clouding our perception of our capabilities, our chances of success and our sense of self-worth. Because they relate to things which have already happened, we may feel we are stuck with them and have to carry them around like a millstone for ever. This is not so. History – as the political world all too readily attests – can be re-written.

Making changes

How might your family life have been improved? What if an ineffectual parent had been more assertive, or a domineering one more approachable? What if your sibling relationships had been different? What if your parents had more money, less money? Suppose they were cleverer, not so clever, more confident, more vulnerable, more ambitious, less ambitious, more attentive, less interfering? Would you rather have attended a different school or lived in a different neighbourhood? What other changes might you make? Given the family history of your choice, how would your life be different now? What image of yourself might you be carrying inside you today?

The fact is, you can make those inner changes by re-inventing a past which replaces discouraging inner images with images and feelings which boost your self-esteem. The so-called reality of the situation is immaterial. Family histories are highly subjective. Each member will have their own version. Even siblings close in age and ostensibly brought up in the same circumstances may argue about what really happened. Over time, facts become distorted and family myths abound. So why not perpetuate the myth of your choosing – one which will nourish and sustain you rather than cause you regret? This does not imply disloyalty to those involved. We can acknowledge with respect and compassion all that occurred in our family, while looking to our invented inner family to support us.

The object of the exercise is *to alter the way we feel about ourselves*. High self-esteem then becomes our point of entry to the assertiveness cycle as described in Chapter 1.

Exercise 4: Changing the energies of your inner family

- Choose an age at which you found family life particularly difficult. Take yourself back to that time. Who or what do you feel is the main source of your problems?

- What things need to be different in order for you to have the family life you want? How far back in your history do you need to go to set those changes in motion? For example, might changes need to be made in your parents' family of origin?

● Go back as far as you need or are able to, and rewrite your story. Take your time. Think it through thoroughly. Notice the effect on the behaviour and personalities of each member of your inner family as the changes are made.

● How do you feel now?

A number of workshop participants who have done this exercise have found that it altered their perception of their outer family. Visualising the enabling effects which the changes would have on their relatives made them realise they were not the only ones who were disadvantaged by the previous situation. In some cases their own energy shifts have been followed by actual changes within the families concerned.

GOING BACK TO SCHOOL

School is a place where most of us have felt intimidated or humiliated at one time, and probably used submissive, aggressive or manipulative behaviour to get by. As adults, any situation which reminds us of school may trigger these behaviour patterns. Our boss asks to see us, a neighbour looks like the class bully, a senior colleague raises one eyebrow like a certain teacher used to – and the fearful child within us is activated.

Re-empowering your inner child
In Exercise 4, we rewrote our family history in order to change the way we felt about ourselves. Similarly, we can re-empower our fearful **inner child** by returning to a time when we felt intimidated, and creating a new version in which we behave assertively.

Exercise 5: Standing up for your self
You will need a pencil and plain paper.

● Think of a situation at school when you felt really intimidated or humiliated. Take time to picture it in some detail. How old were you? Where did it happen?

● Who was the main aggressor? What did they say and do? Who else was involved?

● When you have the scene clearly in your mind *draw what happened*. Notice your feelings as you draw.

● When you have finished your drawing, describe it out loud in the first person present tense, including your feelings as they were at the time; eg 'I am standing in the playground and I can see . . . and it feels as though . . . '. It would be particularly helpful if you could describe it to another person.

● What would you say to your aggressor if you could speak to them now?

● What would you like to have been able to say and do as a child? Take some time to think this out carefully so that it will be really effective.

● Re-run the scene in your imagination, behaving and speaking as you would like to have done at the time. Act it out physically if you want to.

● Play some of the other parts too and notice how that feels.

● Re-draw your picture if you want to.

● Notice how you feel at the end of this exercise.

Additional techniques used in this exercise

Drawing the scene before describing it in words
This puts us in touch with the feeling of being a child again. Also, we are inclined to be more truthful when we draw because we are less proficient in that medium than we are with words.

Telling the story in the present tense
This gives it more immediacy and again puts us more closely in touch with the feelings involved.

Playing all the parts
This gives us a different perspective and can help us to understand some of the characters we have been carrying around inside us.

FORGETTING WHAT YOU LEARNED

Wiping off the old messages

As a result of some of your life experiences, you may have taken on board a number of self-defeating messages of which you are hardly aware until they are verbalised. These may be in serious conflict with your need to assert yourself. Look at the list of self-sabotaging beliefs in Figure 4. Do any of these apply to you? Can you think of any other such hidden messages which might be impeding your progress?

As with the self-assessment statements and the non-verbal behaviours, try to work out where these messages have come from. Are they inherited? Are they defences you learned in order to cope with certain situations? Are they any use to you now? How might they be hindering you? What changes would you like to make?

● Use the exercises and techniques described above to help you make these changes on an inner level.

Clearing old programs

Like self-sabotaging beliefs, old programs are behaviours and attitudes which we have unwittingly taken on board. They may or may not have been useful at one time, but now they tend to take over and run us. Sometimes they reveal themselves in statements which begin 'I always' or 'I never' (go to bed with wet hair, put washing out on a Sunday, trust men with earrings, etc). Or you might find yourself on automatic pilot, ironing a shirt a certain way, leaving something on your plate 'for manners', avoiding wearing blue with green although you rather like it.

Another way in which old programs announce themselves is when we react inappropriately to a person or a situation and wonder – probably with some embarrassment – why on earth we did that. Who or what in the past elicited a response like that, and why has it come to the surface now?

We need to separate the old programs which are still useful from those which are not, and to alter or discard the latter. This can take a great deal of patience. At first we find ourselves saying 'I did it again', then 'I'm doing it again', then 'I almost did it again'. Eventually we can say 'I used to do that', and finally we can forget it altogether.

I should try to be nice
I need people to like me
I must steer clear of conflict
I should not talk about my achievements.
I have no achievements
I should be more feminine
I should be more masculine
I could never take charge
I must not be selfish
I must never hurt anyone
I should not get angry
I must not show I am hurt
I must never appear vulnerable
I must put on a brave face
I should not show that I like somebody
I should never show my feelings
I could never make the first move
I cannot take risks
I cannot ask for what I want
My needs are not important

I might be rejected
I might be criticised
I might be thought unfeminine
I might seem pushy
I might seem too emotional
I might look silly
People might take advantage of me
People might say I'm neurotic
People might hate me
People might like me
Nobody will understand

I can't handle criticism
I can't handle rejection
I can't handle failure
I can't handle conflict
I can't handle change
I can't handle losing
I can't handle winning
I can't handle hurting someone
I can't handle not being liked
I can't handle being liked
I must know where I stand

Fig. 4. Self-sabotaging beliefs.

CHECKLIST

● Becoming assertive involves changing the way you feel about your-self.

● Inner changes can bring about changes in our outer world.

● You can change your self image by changing your inner family.

● Being assertive means deciding what is right for you rather than going along with what you have been told.

● Using your imagination to replay a childhood scene assertively can re-empower your inner child.

Remember, any struggles you have had in the past will be futile if you use them as an excuse. By working with them as suggested, you can use them as a springboard to the future.

ASSERTIVENESS TECHNIQUES

As your confidence grows, you might like to try some simple techniques which will help you behave more assertively. Two examples follow. It would be helpful to rehearse them a few times with a friend before trying them out in a real situation.

The first technique can be useful when somebody is being critical. It also buys you some thinking time.

Asking for clarification

If somebody catches you off guard with a derogatory remark, rather than wilting or becoming defensive you can calmly ask them to explain what they mean.

● 'Can you say what it is about my appearance that you find unac-ceptable?'

● 'What is it about my idea that you find ridiculous?'

● 'Exactly what is it about my behaviour that upsets you?'

Asking somebody to be specific is a particularly good tactic to use when they are letting off steam at your expense. Imagine the effect it might have had on the teacher or bully you confronted in Exercise 5.

The next technique is a step-by-step formula for negotiating a specific change in somebody's behaviour. It can be particularly effective in situations where you find the person in question somewhat intimidating.

The three-stage message

1. **Identify the behaviour** which you find unacceptable. Be very specific. 'When you get angry with me' or 'When you start throwing your weight about' is too vague. What *exactly* is it that gets to you – the shouting, the unacceptable proximity, a certain gesture? Think this out well in advance.

2. **State the effect** this behaviour has on you. Again, be very specific.

3. **Ask for the change** you would like.

Examples

- 'When you wag your finger, I feel like a child and I get tongue-tied. I would like you to keep your hands still when you talk to me.'

- 'When you shout I find I can't think straight. Please could you talk more quietly so that I can concentrate on what you are saying.'

- 'When you leave things lying around, I feel as though you don't care about our home and that upsets me. Please tidy up after you.'

Even if the person is not prepared to comply, the behaviour in question often subsides because drawing attention to it reduces its power.

CASE STUDIES

Howard reinvents his parents
Howard desperately needed his parents to acknowledge his distress at being sent away to school. When he tried to visualise this, he found it

difficult to imagine his father as understanding and compassionate. Going back further in time and visualising his father denying his own feelings under similar circumstances made things clearer. As Howard never knew his paternal grandfather, who was killed in action, it was easy to invent him as a warm-hearted parent who enjoyed his son's company and insisted he should be a day pupil rather than a boarder. Howard was amazed at the relaxed, confident father who emerged as a result of this change and who, in turn, refused to send his son away to school. He also placed his mother in a family setting where she was encouraged to express her feelings and opinions. This change in turn had a very positive effect on her relationship with her children. Howard found the exercise helped him to feel better about himself, and he feels this is a good start.

Stella asks for clarification and eventually gets her message across

After rewriting some of her family history, Stella felt brave enough to challenge her father about his aggressive behaviour. Eventually she decided that *asking for clarification* was a technique she could manage. The next time her father began to shout and bluster, she calmly asked him to tell her exactly what it was that was upsetting him and exactly what he would like her to do to put it right. The shouting and blustering stopped for some time.

When it started again, Stella realised that it was the way he thumped the arms of his chair that made her feel nervous. She conveyed this to him in a three-stage message, at the end of which she asked him to put his hands in his lap when he was talking to her. With a great deal of grumbling he complied, and their relationship is currently much improved as a result.

Andrew thought school was a doddle

Andrew could not see the point of revisiting his school days. He had no problems. School was a 'doddle'. He never has any bother in the playground or the classroom because most people – adults included – were afraid to challenge him.

When he looked at this more closely, however, he was surprised and shocked to realise that he had a lot of enemies and very few friends. This discovery made him decide to replay a few incidents and to imagine himself behaving assertively rather than aggressively. He had to ask Sandra to help with this, as he found he had no idea what to do or say. In the end he had to admit he had found the exercise both thought-provoking and helpful.

SKILLS PRACTICE

1. Think of a current situation in which you feel disempowered by somebody.

2. What exactly do they do which causes you to feel at a disadvantage?

3. Work out a three-stage message indicating:
    a) What they do.
    b) The effect it has on you.
    c) The change you would like.

4. Write the message down and practise it in front of a mirror or with a friend.

5. When you feel confident enough, give your message verbally to the person concerned.

6. How did it go? How did they react? How do you feel now?

3

Being Assertive in Key Relationships
1: Your Family of Origin

During our formative years, we take on board a whole kit-bag of family attitudes and behaviours. From the way our family unit operates, we form a picture of what life is about and what has to be done in order to survive it. Aggressive, manipulative or passive responses to certain situations may be learned as **coping strategies** at this stage. Many of these early impressions and habitual responses may be unwittingly carried forward into adult life. Childhood observations of the adults in our family may also influence our expectations of what life will be like for us in the future. Again, we may carry these expectations forward into adulthood.

GROWING UP

What was life like for you in your formative years? How did your family unit function? Did if feel good to be part of it? Who was in charge? Who did the disciplining? Who did you go to with a problem? Who did you go to when you were ill or hurt? What messages did you get about being a man or a woman, and about how a man or a woman should behave? What models did you have for assertiveness?

Check the characteristic behaviours of your **significant adults** against the list of non-verbal behaviour signals in Figure 3. Which of the four main behaviour types does each of them display most? Was their behaviour the same outside the home as inside it? If not, how and in which circumstances did it change? Do you find yourself following any of these behaviour patterns?

● Knowing the origins of our attitudes and behaviours can be helpful when we are working towards change.

Looking at the way your family functioned

Virginia Satir, family therapist and author of *Peoplemaking*, studied family relationships in four main areas: self-esteem, communication, family rules and interaction with the rest of society.

In troubled families she found that self-esteem was generally lacking, that communication tended to be indirect, vague and not really honest, and that rules were inflexible, permanent and not open to negotiation. She found that interaction with the world outside the family unit tended to involve fear, placation and blame.

In family units which were enabling and nurturing, she described self-esteem as generally high, communication as 'direct, clear, specific and honest', and rules as 'flexible, human, appropriate and subject to change'. She described such families' interaction with society as 'open and hopeful'.

Which of these descriptions best fits your family of origin? Which aspects of your family's style might have helped you to develop assertiveness and which might have prevented this? What changes might have helped you?

● Take some time to imagine your family life as it would have been had those changes been made. Notice the effect this new regime has on you.

Looking at roles that might have been played
Can you think of any particular roles you and other members of your family might have played? Did you ever describe each other in those terms? For example:

● peace maker

● sensible one

● clever one

● sick one

● crazy one

● dependable one

● rebel

● favourite

● Mummy's boy/Daddy's girl

● earth mother

- little helper

- baby

- black sheep

- scapegoat

- fool

- comedian

- victim

- disappointment

- saint.

Some roles – like 'dependable one' and 'baby' – may relate to when each of you arrived on the family scene. Others may have been allocated because there was a vacancy in that department. Such roles, once assumed, tend to stick. Other family members tend to see you and relate to you in that guise rather than as you really are. In due course you might also forget who you are, and become the role. It can take considerable assertiveness to step out of role and bid for recognition in your own right.

How do you feel about any roles you may have assumed in your family? Did they have advantages? What if you had refused those roles and insisted on being seen as you really were – how would that have been? How might your family have reacted?

- Take some time to imagine yourself, your parents and your siblings, if any, relating to each other directly and honestly, without roles.

Looking at the way your family communicated

Virginia Satir identified four conversation styles which people use to protect themselves from rejection, responsibility and conflict. She called these styles placating, blaming, computing and distracting. A placater tries to defuse conflict, a blamer finds fault, thus shifting responsibility away from themselves, a computer disengages emotionally by intellectualising, and a distracter confuses the issue with irrelevant material. To these might be added: copping out, blocking, acting helpless and playing dumb. Can you think of any others?

In families with poor communication skills, each member tends to favour a particular style and to assume it as a role in family discussions. In your family discussions who might habitually have said something like:

> 'It's OK. I know you didn't mean to be nasty.'
> 'Can't you do anything properly!'
> 'Suppose we consider a hypothetical scenario.'
> 'What's the use? It won't get us anywhere.'
> 'Ask someone else.'
> 'I refuse to answer that.'
> 'It's all so confusing.'
> 'Is anyone hungry?'

Have you ever found yourself favouring any of these conversational roles?

● Imagine your family of origin having a discussion in which each member behaves and speaks assertively rather than assuming a conversational role. What effect does this have on you?

CHECKLIST

The way your family of origin operated may still be influencing your:

● self-esteem

● attitudes

● behaviour

● communication style

● confidence when interacting with others

● ability to be assertive

● ability to be yourself rather than assuming a role.

WORKING WITH YOUR INNER FAMILY

In Chapter 2 we saw how changing the energies of your inner family could have a positive effect on the way you feel about yourself, and the way you behave as a result. We also saw how these inner changes could help to bring about here-and-now changes in the dynamics of the outer family.

The next exercise is designed to follow on from exercises 1-4 in that chapter. It is longer and more detailed, and works specifically on family roles, relationship and communication. It uses the technique of viewing episodes from the past as though they are taking place on a stage. This allows a degree of detachment from the emotional content so that changes may be made more objectively.

As with the exercises in Chapter 2, the questions and instructions should be read onto a tape, leaving suitable pauses for your response. Before playing back the tape, it would be extremely helpful for you to recall each of those earlier exercises, consulting any notes you made at the time.

Exercise: Staging a family discussion

Close your eyes – and imagine you are in a theatre. The curtain is down. The play will be beginning soon. It will be about a family discussion which affected your life badly – a discussion in which you now wish you could have behaved and spoken differently. The play will be in two acts. The first act will have two scenes. Scene 1 will show the events leading up to that family discussion. Scene 2 will show the discussion itself.

Who will be in the cast? Where will these two scenes be taking place?

Act 2 will have three scenes: the rewritten version of act 1, plus a final scene to show the new outcome. You will have the chance to write this act in the interval.

And now, the lights dim in the theatre . . . the curtains open . . . you see the scene and the characters . . . and act 1 begins. Watch now as the events which lead up to that significant family discussion begin to unfold.

pause for at least two minutes

And now it is time for the curtain to come down on scene 1. Before the next scene, take some time to think about what you have seen and heard. Did you notice yourself or any other family members assuming a familiar role rather than being themselves? Think carefully about any changes you would like to make to this scene when you rewrite it.

pause

And now it is time for scene 2 to begin. The lights dim, the curtains open. Where are you in this scene? Who is about to speak? Watch as the discussion which is to have such an affect on your life unfolds.

pause for at least two minutes

And now it is time for the curtain to come down on scene 2. Again – take some time to think about what you have seen and heard. Did you notice yourself or any other family member falling into a conversational style rather than actively listening and discussing? Think carefully about how you would like to rewrite this discussion.

And now it is time to go backstage and discuss the changes to scenes 1 and 2 with the cast. In act 2 you will be appearing on stage with them. Tell them to drop their old roles and be themselves. Show them how to communicate assertively – being honest about feelings and genuinely looking for solutions which will meet everybody's needs.

pause for at least two minutes

You will need new programme notes and advertising posters for this act. See your name and the name of each family member in big letters saying 'Starring x y z as him/herself!'. Notice how that feels.

pause

And now it is time for act 2 to begin, so take your place on stage. The curtains open . . . and the new scene 1 begins. How do you feel as you take part in this new version?

pause for at least two minutes

And now it is time for the curtain to come down on scene 1. How are you feeling? Is there anything you need to say to other family members before the next scene?

And it is time for scene 2 to begin. This is the new style family discussion. Move to your place on the stage . . . The curtains open . . . and the discussion begins. How do you feel in your new role? How do the other family members respond to you, and you to them? You might like to try playing some of the other parts and see how that feels.

pause for as long as required

And now it is time for the curtain to come down on scene 2. How do you feel after that family discussion? How does this differ from your feelings after other family discussions in the past?

Scene 3 is going to be about what happens as a result of this discussion. Take some time to work it out with the other family members. It may be a long scene spanning several years of your life. Take as long as you need to think it through.

pause

When you are ready, take your place on the stage. The curtain rises and scene 3 begins to unfold. Notice all the changes in your feelings and behaviour. Notice the differences in your family members as they respond to the new situation.

pause

As you come to the end of this scene, you notice that the auditorium is full of people. You walk to the front of the stage and take a bow as the audience clap and cheer. Your new play is a definite hit.

When you are ready, allow the curtain to come down and the lights to dim. Say anything you need to say to the rest of the cast, and take your leave of them.

Return to the present, open your eyes and make any notes you need to make.

● Which worked best for you, watching the play or taking part in it? You can apply either method to future exercises in this book.

● Think of suitable titles for this play and its individual acts.

CHANGING THE DYNAMICS OF YOUR OUTER FAMILY

Whatever our age, there may still be left-over feelings from childhood which put us at a disadvantage when dealing with certain family members. There may be someone you still find so intimidating that you get tongue-tied when you meet, or someone you feel unable to be honest with because they are easily shocked, or a very critical family member in whose presence you feel worthless, or one who seems so needy that you feel unable to say 'no' to their demands.

These are uncomfortable reactions which interfere with our ability to assert ourselves with that family member – and possibly with anyone who reminds us of them. If we want to change this, we will need to address the situation with the person concerned. This is likely to have one of three outcomes.

1. They may prove not to be particularly intimidating, shockable, crit-

ical or needy, but just an average person to whom you were reacting from a child position (like meeting one of your childhood teachers and feeling you should call them 'sir' or 'miss').

2. They may habitually behave in any of the aggressive or manipulative ways described above, and addressing this with them might start a process of change.

3. They may habitually behave aggressively or manipulatively and not be prepared to change – in which case you will need to replace your childish reaction with an adult and assertive one.

Opening negotiations

As discussed in Chapter 2, there are a number of simple techniques which can help us to behave more assertively. They can be very useful in getting us past the initial fear of approaching someone to whom we find it difficult to relate. (Although we are talking mainly about family problems at present these techniques can, of course, be used in any situation.)

The technique recommended for use when someone is being critical was **asking for clarification**. This can also be used when somebody's seeming neediness leaves us feeling unable to say 'no'. Unless they are specific about their needs, we know only that they 'need us' – which can feel quite overwhelming. It can be very useful to ask: 'What exactly would you like me to do for you?' Once needs have been identified, you can say whether you are able to meet them or not.

The technique recommended for use when you feel intimidated was **three-stage message**. Remember, it is important to identify exactly the aspect of the person's behaviour which you find disturbing.

This technique can be used when something a person says or does 'pushes your buttons'. For example, to someone who is not specific about their needs you might say: 'When you phone me up and just cry, I feel completely helpless. Could you tell me what you need so that I can tell you whether I can help?'

Clarifying the situation

In a situation where you are unsure whether it is the person's behaviour or your inappropriate reaction which is causing the problem (see 1. above) use only steps one and two of the three-stage message, *ie* **identify the behaviour which you find unacceptable** and **state the effect this behaviour has on you**. This leaves room for any misunderstandings to be cleared up.

TRYING NEW TECHNIQUES

1. Expressing the dilemma

This is a useful way of checking out someone else's feelings or reactions. Sometimes we may find we are going round in circles conversing with ourselves along the lines of, 'If I do this, she might feel that . . . On the other hand, if I don't do it she might think . . .' A better use of our time and energy would be to express the dilemma to the person concerned and find out what they really feel or think. For example, in the case of the family member who we thought was easily shocked we could say: 'Sometimes I get the feeling that I've shocked you, and then I feel anxious about telling you things. Would you rather I avoided certain subjects?'

2. Owning the feelings

This is really a principle rather than a technique. Basically it means taking responsibility for your own feelings and not blaming them on a person or a situation. Instead of saying 'You make me/it makes me feel', say 'When you do this/when this happens, I feel.' This is just a statement, and does not necessarily require the other person to respond.

3. Selective agreement

This is another technique which is useful when somebody is being critical. Instead of being manipulated into feeling negative, making excuses or engaging in a row, you agree with any truth you can find in their statement.

> 'Yes, I am untidy sometimes.'
> 'You're right. I might regret not taking an umbrella.'
> 'Yes, your opinions about children's behaviour are very different from mine.'

If you can find no truth in the statement, say 'I don't see it that way' or 'We obviously have different views. What can we do about that?'

MANAGING CHANGE

When any family relationship changes, it can make adjustments necessary in other parts of the system – especially where the people involved have been seen in a particular role. A hitherto full-time caregiver may decide to pursue a career, a divorced or widowed parent may remarry, a dependent relative may find a way to be independent, someone who has suffered in silence may find the courage to speak their mind. All these scenarios have implications for those who are close to the people concerned.

How might your new attitudes and behaviour affect various members of your family? How might they react? How will you handle that? Managing the knock-on effects may require as much assertiveness as the original changes. The five techniques you have practised so far will be helpful in this process. If in doubt as to which one to use, express the dilemma. Say 'I'm not sure how to handle this. I'll need to think about it' and give yourself time to do so.

CHECKLIST

Changes in family dynamics may:

- be brought about through inner work

- occur through addressing problems with the people concerned

- have a knock-on effect

- help to change the way you relate to people outside the family.

CASE STUDIES

Howard's family did not communicate

When Howard recalled the family discussions about his schooling, he realised they were not really discussions at all. Whenever he tried to express his feelings, his father blamed his mother for molly-coddling him. His mother tried to placate them both, telling his father that she knew he was right, and assuring Howard that the school holidays would soon come. As Howard became more and more distressed, his father would go into computing mode, quoting statistics to prove the benefits of boarding school for boys of his age. His mother would then try to distract with irrelevant comments about 'proper meals' and putting name-tags in his clothes. Although his parents are deceased and he could not address this with them in reality, he was able to rewrite the final crucial discussion so that proper communication took place and he did not have to go to boarding school. He found this a healing experience.

Stella's family were low on self-esteem

Stella's father's family considered he had 'married beneath him'. They treated his wife and children with ill-disguised contempt, which made him defensive and resentful. Stella's mother felt increasingly 'not good enough' and communicated these feelings to her three daughters. Stella remembers visits to her father's family as fraught with anxiety that she would 'show herself up'. Despite this history, her father's two surviving sisters expect her to do shopping and other errands for them and are critical rather than appreciative of her efforts. She put up with this for a number of years. Then she realised that they saw her in the role of unpaid servant rather than as a person in her own right. This made her angry enough to tell them that the situation was unacceptable, and to assertively state her terms for change. They must either pay her a domestic's wages or treat her as a member of the family. Otherwise they must find someone else to run their errands. She has given them a week to decide.

Andrew sees anyone outside his family as a threat

Andrew had always thought of himself as coming from a close family. Now he thinks of his family of origin as a *closed* family. He realises that he grew up thinking of anyone who was not a family member as an outsider to be viewed with suspicion. In school the same attitude applied to his gang – which was largely composed of family members. He was often involved in playground fights as a result. Later he had the same feelings of family loyalty towards his rugby team and was involved in several brawls with rival teams and their supporters. He now recognises this behaviour as a response to early family conditioning, and is trying to change it. Replacing his early role models with others which are more suitable is proving helpful.

GETTING THE MOST FROM THIS CHAPTER

1. Spend as much time as possible on the family exercises. Do the shorter ones more than once to get extra insight.

2. Practise the new assertiveness techniques with a friend before using them for real.

3. Focus on one of the techniques each day and use it whenever appropriate.

4. Choose a family situation which needs to be resolved and work on it.

5. Record all your results and your thoughts about them in your progress journal.

4

Being Assertive in Key Relationships
2: Your Family Now

In Chapter 3 we looked at how a 'kit-bag' of family attitudes and behaviours might have been acquired during our formative years. These attitudes and behaviours would have been learned in order to survive within that particular family unit at that time. As adults we will have discarded some of them, and consciously retained others. Some, however, may be so ingrained that they operate without our being aware of it. Many of them – even ones we thought we had discarded – may be triggered when we set up a family unit of our own. If we are single, we might find ourselves transferring them onto friendships or groups to which we belong.

An important part of the process of becoming assertive is to identify and work through any elements of old programs which intrude on your life in this way.

UNPACKING YOUR FAMILY KIT-BAG

When a couple sets up home together, two family kit-bags will need to be unpacked and the contents evaluated, along with everything else each of them brings to the relationship. The contents of both may prove to be very similar, which could be a source of comfort or tension depending on the circumstances; or they may be intriguingly different, or different in ways which make the partners begin to feel alienated.

Whatever the case, decisions will need to be made about the future of each item. Some will have to be shelved, or discarded. Should the relationship eventually break down, each partner will probably carry away a kit-bag which is rather different from the one with which they arrived.

Making your findings
If you were to unpack your current kit-bag, what would you find? Think about:

- the basic principles you live by

- how you would define a good relationship

- how you and your partner communicate

- how you organise and share domestic tasks

- how you organise your finances

- how you go about sorting out problems

- whether you discuss problems with friends or keep them to yourselves

- where you stand regarding religion and politics

- your views on child rearing.

If you dug a little deeper, what other recipes for living might come to light?

Do your answers to these questions signify a well thought out and consciously implemented approach to life, or have you inherited some of these attitudes and behaviours from your family or origin and not really thought to question them? Are the items in your current kit-bag different from the ones you brought to your present or most recent relationship? If so, how have they changed? Who or what brought those changes about? Are you happy with this?

If your answer to the last question is 'no' you may feel it is time to assert yourself in order to negotiate for the changes you want.

Discussing your findings with your partner

If your partner is willing, ask them to unpack their family kit-bag as above. Take some time to compare your answers and talk through the implications.

As a couple, discuss how satisfied you are with your relationship. Perhaps your childhood experiences have given each of you different expectations, which need to be identified and talked through. Do you sometimes find yourselves behaving just like your parents, perhaps casting each other in particular roles which will reinforce this? Role playing interferes with real person-to-person communication and is therefore a barrier to assertiveness. Discuss how you might help each other to shed these roles so that you can be yourselves and relate more honestly.

Maybe you find the very thought of being like your parents so horrifying that you always strive to do the opposite. This is also a non-assertive position – a reaction to a past situation, rather than a positive step taken as a person in your own right.

Comparing your original family with your family now

In terms of Virginia Satir's four measures of family relationship, how would you describe your present family or partnership's:

- levels of self-esteem

- styles of communication

- system of rules

- way of interacting with the rest of society?

Does your family unit function in ways you have consciously chosen? Does it feel good to be part of it? Who is in charge? If you have children, who do they go to with a problem or if they are ill or hurt? Who does the disciplining? What messages are your children getting about being male/female and about how males/females behave? What models do they have for assertiveness?

- How did you answer these questions re your family of origin in Chapter 3? Are any of the answers similar? Are you still running some old family programs?

- Discuss your answers with your partner. Talk about any changes you would like to make.

Learning to be yourself in all relationships

As discussed earlier, old family programs may also be triggered when you find yourself in certain group situations, eg at work, on a committee, or as a member of an organisation. In such situations you might find yourself playing any number of familiar family roles, from mother to underdog. You might also find yourself reacting in ways which are inappropriate to the current circumstances. If this happens, step back and try to look objectively at the person you are interacting with. Who do they remind you of?

- One way to get past that false identity and interact with the real person behind it, is to list all the ways in which they are *unlike* the person they remind you of.

CHECKLIST

Some common barriers to assertiveness within a relationship are:

- following old family programming

- having incompatible expectations

- role casting and role playing

- behaving like your parents

- trying not to behave like your parents

- projecting another person's characteristics onto your partner.

DEFINING YOUR ROLE

How would you describe your role or roles within your present family unit? Are people used to relying on you? Do you find yourself making most of the decisions? Or is yours a more passive role? Do you find it hard to say no? If someone says 'I'd love a cup of tea', do you feel obliged to make it for them? If not, how do you respond? Are you thought of as not particularly capable? Are others critical of you and do you accept this as your due?

Are there any advantages to assuming these roles? Are there any similarities to roles you may have played in your family of origin? Are you reliving your past? Are you happy with the present situation?

Changing the way your family sees you

If you want to change the way you operate within your family unit, you will also need to change the family's perceptions of you and your roles.

- Start by **expressing the dilemma** and **owning the feelings** (Chapter 3).

- If someone's attitude or behaviour makes this difficult, identify exactly what they do which upsets you, then use the **three-stage message** (Chapter 2).

- If people are critical of the changes you want to make, **ask for clarification** (Chapter 2) or use **selective agreement** (Chapter 3).

Examples

Expressing the dilemma/owning the feelings
'We've got into the habit of me cooking and you washing up so it might

be hard to change that – but I really would like to have a meal cooked for me sometimes.'

Three-stage message
'When you look all crestfallen like that, I feel guilty and I feel I shouldn't be asking you to do it. Could you try to look more positive about it.'

Asking for clarification
'Exactly what is it about the thought of cooking that upsets you?'

Selective agreement
'Yes you do other jobs around the house.' This could be followed by the **recorded announcement,** 'but I really would like to have a meal cooked for me sometimes.' (See below.)

TRYING A NEW TECHNIQUE

Recorded announcement
To get your point across in the face of strong opposition:

1. **State** your case in as few words as possible.

2. **Listen** to what the other person has to say and acknowledge it.

3. **Repeat** your original statement in the same words – like a recorded announcement.

Example
'I don't want to make this decision by myself. I want you to help me. Yes, I realise you have got a lot on your mind right now – but I don't want to make this decision by myself. I want you to help me. I know you trust my judgement – but I don't want to make this decision by myself . . .' etc.

- If the other person raises a distracting side issue, **acknowledge** it without being deflected from your purpose. Say something like: 'We can talk about that as soon as we settle this.'

- If the other person does not seem to be hearing or understanding, ask them to **repeat back** what you have said. Say something like: 'What do you think I am asking you to do?'

Can you identify any specific roles played by others in your family unit – partner, children, step-children? How do you feel about that? Use the techniques described above to help you level with them.

ASSERTING YOURSELF AS A PARENT

Heavy-handed authoritarian styles of child-rearing are, thankfully, no longer in fashion. Acceptable alternatives are still a matter of debate, which leaves many parents wondering just how they should proceed.

In the absence of role models or guidelines, many find themselves relating to their children aggressively, passively or manipulatively rather than being assertive. How would you describe your own behaviour in this respect? When not getting the co-operation you want from your children might you:

1.   Threaten them with a good smacking.

2.   Ignore what they are doing and hope they will grow out of it.

3.   Tell them you are sure Prince Harry doesn't behave like that.

Or are you able to deal with most situations confidently, while respecting their viewpoints and feelings? (Assertiveness self-assessment, Chapter 1.) Look again at that Assertiveness self-assessment. Which other items do you think particularly important in the context of parenting? How high did you score on those items? Which ones need more work?

At times when your relationship with your children requires more assertiveness, the assertiveness techniques so far described can be very useful.

● **Expressing the dilemma** and **owning the feelings** are always good starting points.

● **Asking for clarification** and **selective agreement** are useful for not getting hooked by a critical or hurtful remark. 'What exactly do you mean when you say this dinner is yukky?' 'Yes, I do get grumpy sometimes.'

● **Three-stage message** and **recorded announcement** are both useful when requesting a behaviour change.

- Remember to check your **non-verbal behaviour signals** (see Chapter 1) to make sure you are not giving conflicting messages.

Asking for time

This can be a very useful habit to cultivate, particularly for parents. Most children are very good at springing requests on us when we are preoccupied, which can leave us momentarily stuck for something to say other than 'no' or 'all right then', either of which we may regret later. This mental gap can be bridged by getting into the habit of saying 'I need to think about that', and then stating a time for giving your decision. The latter is important because it sets clear boundaries around the situation and helps to prevent your being constantly pestered during the intervening period.

This is a simple enough strategy, but it needs to be practised in order to have it on the tip of your tongue when needed.

CHECKLIST

Assertive parenting requires:

- self-awareness

- confidence

- respect for yourself and your children

- good communication skills

- time and attention

- a few techniques to help you over bumpy bits

- practice.

CASE STUDIES

Howard had cast his wife in a role

Howard realises that he has cast Jenny in the role of 'helpless child', reflecting the helpless child that he once felt himself to be. He has been trying to heal his own past hurts by giving her the love that he so badly wanted then. At first this hooked Jenny's feelings of need for her father, who died when she was in her teens. She was therefore happy to accept Howard's 'fathering' in the early years of their marriage. This situation prevented either of them from seeing the real person behind the role. Now that Jenny is in her 30s and keen to develop as a person in her own right, she and Howard are having to redefine their relationship. Howard is secretly worried that Jenny may not want him any more and might become attracted to a younger man, but he has not yet been able to express this fear to her.

Stella tries it at home

Following the successful confrontations of her father and his sisters, Stella feels more confident about persuading Jeff and her sons to take an active role in the running of the household. She makes a list of the jobs she wants them to do, then asks for a family discussion to decide how those tasks should be divided. At first everyone has 'other commitments'. Stella acknowledges this, while using *recorded announcement* to reiterate her need for a meeting. Eventually the discussion takes place. By *expressing the dilemma, owning the feelings* and using *recorded announcement*, Stella is able to state her case. Jeff admits that they have taken her for granted, and somewhat grudgingly helps his sons to divide up the tasks. Stella expects to be asserting herself for some time in order to ensure that they are carried out.

Andrew unpacks his kit-bag

Andrew had thought of himself as an autonomous individual, so he is rather shocked to discover the strong family conditioning behind his general approach to life. When he thought about his relationship, his views, his principles and the way he organises his life, he realises how strongly he has been influenced by his parents. In fact, when he discusses his findings with Sandra she agrees that he could have been talking about his parents' marriage. When she thinks about her family conditioning, she realises that she is strongly influenced by her mother's fear of confrontation. This has led her to take a passive role in the marriage until now. Andrew and Sandra discuss ways in which they can break this pattern and begin to relate on a more equal basis. They realise this will not be easy at first, but they intend to persevere.

SKILLS PRACTICE

1. Choose a particular area of family tension and use the insight gained from Chapters 3 and 4 to help resolve it.

2. Identify some current situations where the assertiveness techniques you have learned would be useful. Practise the appropriate techniques, then try them out.

3. Record your results and your thoughts about them in your progress journal.

5

Behaving Assertively at Work

Whatever work we do, most of us will find it stressful at times. We get overloaded, we have targets and deadlines to meet, unreasonable demands may be made on us, we may have to cope with other people's anger or brusqueness, we may feel taken for granted, we may be horribly bored. These are familiar work hazards which a suitably assertive attitude can help us to weather. However, we may find that in our working environment assertiveness eludes us, leaving us feeling vulnerable, foolish, incapable and unable to speak up for ourselves. It could be that the regime in that establishment is particularly abusive, in which case the assertive act might be to leave. Another quite likely possibility is that we are reacting more strongly than the situation warrants because an 'old tape' is playing – one which triggers memories of a period in our lives when we may often have felt disempowered – our schooldays.

UNPACKING THE WORKPLACE KIT-BAG

Unless we are self-employed, our work situation is likely to have a number of parallels with school. We may sit at a desk or have to wear a uniform – or both. There will be a set of rules we must abide by and a certain amount of work to complete neatly and accurately in an allotted time. There will probably be a number of authority figures in evidence; one may even sit at a front desk watching, as in some typing pools, or patrol the gangways as on the shop floor. Too many toilet breaks, talking and eating at inappropriate times and any form of slacking will be discouraged. We may even find the equivalent of the class sneak, bully or swot among our colleagues.

Triggering feelings and beliefs

When such memories are triggered they can evoke the same emotional response that we had in the past, so causing the additional stress of having to behave as an adult under circumstances in which we are feeling more like a child.

In Chapters 3 and 4 we looked at the kit-bag of family attitudes and behaviours which we may have accumulated as a result of our up-bringing. If we managed to survive school without being expelled, it is probably because we accumulated a similar kit-bag in response to that environment. Now, in order to survive the world of work, we may find ourselves buying into the kit-bag of commonly held beliefs which oper-ates in our particular establishment. Its contents, like those of our earli-er kit-bags, may conflict with our need to be assertive. Eventually some-thing will have to give.

EXPOSING SOME WORKPLACE MYTHS

Figure 5 shows a number of anti-assertiveness workplace 'myths', some or all of which we might find in a work survival kit-bag. The contrary fact – the assertive position – is listed alongside each one. Which myths operate in your workplace? Do you subscribe to some of them? Many of those listed carry echoes of school. How do you feel about this? Would you prefer to adopt an assertive position? If your answer to the last ques-tion is yes, try tackling one myth at a time, starting with the one which affects you most.

- How does it affect your work performance generally?

- When did you last experience its effects directly?

- Exactly what happened?

- How did you feel?

- How would it have felt to make the contrary assertive statement at that time?

- How does it feel to make that contrasting assertive statement now?

Repeat the assertive statement to yourself until you firmly believe it, and feel confident that you could make it aloud at your place of work.

The resultant change in your attitude and behaviour may well get the message across without your having to deliver it verbally. When you feel satisfied with the effect, choose another myth to work on. At times when you feel less confident, you might also find it useful to repeat to yourself the affirmation 'I am an adult, doing an adult's job and doing it well'.

Myth	Fact
Mistakes are not allowed.	You have a right to make mistakes.
You should put the needs of the team first.	You have a right to put yourself first sometimes.
You should be as accommodating as possible so that the workplace will run smoothly.	You have a right to say no.
You should keep your opinions to yourself, especially if you disagree with those in authority.	You have a right to express your opinions and beliefs.
It is best to count your blessings and not rock the boat.	You have a right to negotiate for change.
You should never interrupt.	You have a right to be heard and to interrupt if your voice is being crowded out.
Asking a lot of questions reveals your ignorance.	You have a right to understand what is required of you and what is taking place around you.
If someone take the trouble to give you advice, you should act on it.	You have a right to ignore advice.
You should not bother colleagues with your problems.	You have a right to ask for help.
Never bring personal problems to work.	You have a right to feel and express pain.
If someone brings you a problem you must always do your best to sort it out.	You are not responsible for other people's problems.
You should be sensitive to the needs of others, even when they are not expressed.	Other people have a right and a responsibility to express their own needs.
Anger should never be expressed in the workplace.	You have a right to express your feelings.
Knowing you did something well should be its own reward. It is immature to want praise.	You have a right to receive recognition for your work and achievements. It is human to want appreciation.
You should always be very clear about your reasons for doing things.	You have a right not to justify yourself to others.
You must be prepared to be ruthless – it's a cut-throat world.	Everyone has a right to have their needs respected.

Fig. 5. Anti-assertiveness workplace myths.

Handling opposition

If you meet opposition in making these changes, use **recorded announcement** to reiterate the assertive statement. If you still get a negative reaction and it bothers you, identify the exact words or behaviour which you find problematic (the list of non-verbal signals in Chapter 1 may help) and use **three-stage message** to help you state your case.

Opposition to your newly acquired assertiveness may not be overt. The person or people concerned may signal their disapproval in subtle ways which are difficult to pinpoint but no less obvious. In that case acknowledge inwardly that their behaviour is having an adverse effect on you. Say to yourself, 'This person is behaving aggressively in not respecting my rights. I will continue to behave assertively', and stick to your guns.

Ending power games

Look again at the list of aggressive and manipulative behaviours in Chapter 1. These are all things people may do consciously or unconsciously when jockeying for power. Invasion of territory is another such tactic, and it can take many forms. A colleague might encroach on your workspace with files, trailing plants or other objects. They might frequently become loud and jocular on the telephone so that it grates on your ears and disturbs your concentration. They might lean intrusively across your desk when talking to you. They may borrow your equipment without asking, or not return borrowed items so that you have to go and ask for them. They may come back late when they are supposed to relieve you of your shift.

Using the three-stage message

In such situations, provided the person concerned has similar job status to yours, you can use the three-stage message: Remember to:

- identify exactly how the person concerned is encroaching on your space

- describe the effect this has on you

- ask for the change you want.

The three-stage message will probably not be effective if the person is playing the power game of ignoring you. One company director's regular power move was to summon a colleague to her office, then busily engage herself in a writing task from which she would not look up when they entered. Someone who was getting 'the full treatment' might stand for several minutes by her desk, unacknowledged. How would you handle this situation?

Somebody close to the director in status might be able to deliver a form of three-stage message. A better solution for others might be to say straight away 'I can see you're very busy, I'll come back later' and turn to go. Asking 'Shall I come back later?' or hovering in hope of a reply would be a passive response.

Secretaries who take shorthand often express their frustration at the amount of time wasted while their boss carries on a lengthy phone call in the middle of dictation. They need to be able to leave should such a phone call get underway, or to arrange for phone calls to be diverted or cut short at such times, but may find it difficult to broach this with their boss. A three-stage message referring to the wasted time in terms of its adverse effects on the company, rather than the secretary, often proves helpful in this situation.

TRYING NEW TECHNIQUES

Introducing the five-stage message

This is a more detailed and more formal version of the three-stage message. It is particularly useful in a work situation which requires delivery of complicated or precise feedback. The steps are as follows:

1. **Identify** the other person's problem behaviour.

2. **State** the tangible effect this behaviour has on you.

3. **Say** how you feel about that.

4. **Ask** for the behaviour change you want.

5. **Invite** the other person to comment.

For example:

1. 'When your cash returns are late . . .

2. . . . it oftens means the bank is closed when I get there and I have to keep the money at home overnight.

3. I always feel very uneasy about it.

4.   I would appreciate it if you could cash up earlier.

5.   Will this be a problem for you?'

Recognising old videos

When you find yourself very reluctant to confront a particular colleague, ask yourself whether they remind you of anybody.

Take some time to list the people you have found intimidating or upsetting in your life. Recall some actual incidents involving those people. What exactly did they do? Return to Chapter 2, Going Back to School. Recall the incidents which came up in those exercises. Does this give you further clues?

Does this colleague remind you of any of the people you have just been thinking about, or is there something about the situation which is similar to an event in the past? To help you wipe this old tape so that you can react appropriately to the current person or situation, take some time to think about:

1.   All the ways in which your colleague is *not* like the person from the past.

2.   All the ways in which the present situation differs from the earlier one.

CHECKLIST

Becoming more assertive at work involves:

●   clearing disabling echoes from the past

●   discrediting disempowering workplace myths

●   challenging the attitudes and behaviour of colleagues

●   practising techniques which will help to handle situations confidently.

The assertiveness techniques in this book are useful not only for trouble-shooting, but for generally improving communications with colleagues. Even when you feel reasonably at ease in your working environment and are able to deal with most situations confidently, there are times when specific skills or techniques can smooth the progress of potentially sensitive exchanges – particularly those involving **feedback**.

GIVING AND RECEIVING FEEDBACK

The purpose of feedback, whether positive (praise) or negative (criticism) is to provide the recipient with useful information about themselves or their performance. It is not a vehicle for the venting of the provider's feelings, although these should be stated and owned. Unless an outcome is to be negotiated, it should be left to the recipient to decide whether or not to act on the information. Feedback with an unstated agenda is manipulation.

Giving positive feedback
First, be clear about your motives. Are you aiming to boost the recipient's confidence? Do you genuinely feel they have done a good job and want to let them know this? Are you seeking reciprocal praise, or other return favours? Are you ducking out of saying what you really think? Bearing in mind your motivation, will your delivery of this feedback be an assertive act?

Sound though your motives might be, it can still be difficult to give praise without sounding patronising. It helps if you specify the aspects that pleased you. For example, rather than 'You did a good job of chairing that meeting', say something like 'I was impressed by the way you handled those questions about x, and those anecdotes about y really helped to lighten the atmosphere.' This shows you have been paying attention and that your appreciation is genuine.

Giving negative feedback
This is a potential minefield which many people avoid by not confronting others unless absolutely forced to. It is certainly a test of developing assertiveness skills. Feedback should never be presented so tentatively or apologetically or wrapped up in qualifying statements that the message is lost.

It has to be accepted that there is no way in which constructive critical feedback can be given so that the recipient feels happy about it. You can only aim for a sensitively pitched exchange in which the recipient is able to hear the message without feeling under attack.

Again, the first rule is to be very clear about your motives in giving this message. Is this about venting your feelings, or is it a genuine piece of constructive criticism which could be of use to the recipient? If the latter, do you want the outcome to be a change in the recipient's behaviour? If you do, use the three- or five-stage message. Otherwise, as skillfully and sensitively as possible and without judging or labelling, tell the recipient how you perceive their behaviour and how you feel about it.

Remember

● Your task is to present your feedback as skillfully and sensitively as you can.

● The recipient's task is to handle his/her feelings about what you have said.

● You are responsible for your part of the transaction.

● You are not responsible for the recipient's reaction.

Provided you have proceeded with care and integrity, you have no reason to feel guilty if the recipient is angry or upset (although it can be difficult not to).

SKILLS PRACTICE

How would you word your feedback in the following situations?

1. A colleague frequently makes sexist remarks. You want them to know how you feel about this and to change their behaviour.

2. A local firm has made an excellent job of redesigning your office, and has also charged much less than a bigger company would have done.

3. One of the typists is producing very badly laid out and misspelled letters, and seems unaware of this.

4. You are aware that a colleague is stealing small items from the company on a fairly regular basis. Nobody else knows about this.

5. A colleague's phone manner is very brusque, and this is alienating customers.

Handling valid criticism

The first step is to check whether the criticism is valid, invalid, or a put-down. If it is valid, the next step is to avoid being manipulated through guilt or anxiety into:

a)   shame-faced apologies and promises to make amends, or
b)   defensiveness, denial and counter-criticism.

Instead, you assertively accept your short-comings *in that situation*. (Do not get hooked into 'I am a bad/useless person.'). If appropriate, focus on how the situation might be rectified.

Example
    'You were late back from lunch.'
    'Yes, I was.'

If the critic has not been affected by your lateness, this is enough. Otherwise add something like 'I could stay later this evening.' If the other person makes a general accusation rather than a specific criticism, agree with any truth in their statement.

Example
    'You're never here on time.'
    'I am late today.'

If you can find no truth in the statement say, 'I don't experience it that way', or 'We seem to view this differently. What can we do about that?' You may wish to enquire as to the other person's interest in criticising you. 'I am late today. How does that affect you?'

Handling invalid criticism

If the criticism is clearly **invalid**, say so without apology or explanation.

    'You've really been slacking today.'
    'I disagree. I have not been slacking.'

You could also ask for clarification.

    'What is it exactly that makes you say I've been slacking?'

Handling a put-down

If the criticism is a put-down, you could either ask for clarification, or disagree and also respond assertively to the put-down.

Examples
    'You look an absolute mess.'
    'What exactly is it about my appearance that you dislike?'
    or 'I disagree. I do not look a mess and I feel angry with your put-down.'

A less confrontative way of handling criticism, valid or invalid, is to calmly agree that there *may* be some truth in what the critic has just said.

Examples
    'You've made a complete pig's ear of this report.'
    'Perhaps it's not the best report I've ever done.'
    'You're the rudest person I've ever met.'
    'I might be a bit outspoken sometimes.'

This halts the exchange by giving the critic nothing to feed off.

Handling praise
Sometimes it can feel as difficult to accept appreciation as it is to accept criticism. We may try to avoid embarrassment by diminishing our achievements. An assertive response would be to agree with the appreciative comment.

    'Thank you. I'm pleased with what I did, too.' or 'I'm glad you like it.'
    Or you could ask for clarification.
    'Thank you. What was it about my presentation that you liked?'

WORKING FOR WIN-WIN SOLUTIONS

In assertive exchanges there should be no winners and losers, no top-dog and under-dog. The aim is for both sides to be able to express their needs and rights calmly, while respecting the needs and rights of the other. The techniques described – particularly the constructive handling of feedback – can be used to negotiate **win-win solutions** and mutually acceptable compromises.

●   Pay attention to any emotional response you may have to the other person. Both positive and negative responses can interfere with your ability to engage actively with the process.

- If you feel irritated with the other person, make an effort to focus on what you have in common with them. Remember, the goal is to accomplish something together, not to have an argument.

CHECKLIST

Feedback, whether positive or negative:

- is for the benefit of the recipient

- should be given sensitively

- if positive, should be agreed with and maybe clarified

- if negative, should be assessed for its validity

- should be agreed with calmly and clarified if valid

- should be disagreed with calmly if invalid

- can be deflected by partial agreement

- can be a useful tool in negotiating win-win solutions.

CASE STUDIES

Howard's line manager reminds him of his English teacher

Howard reports to his line manager, a woman, every Thursday afternoon and has come to dread these meetings. When he analyses his fears they seem rather unreasonable as his manager is generally appreciative of his work and seldom has any adverse comments to make. Returning to a visualisation of his school days, however, he realises that she has similar colouring and build to an English teacher who used to be extremely scathing about his poor spelling. Furthermore, by an ironic coincidence, Thursday was the day that detentions were held at his school, and he was frequently kept in on Thursday afternoons to copy out endless corrections of misspelled words. After Howard realises that his dread of Thursday afternoons is an echo from the past, it gradually subsides. He even begins to see the funny side of it. Eventually he is able to share the joke with his manager, who is very pleased that the previously inexplicable tension between them has now eased.

Stella improves her working conditions

Stella has made caring for home and family her full-time occupation. She feels it generates stress which is similar to that encountered in other places of work. Overloading, deadlines and unreasonable demands, plus feeling under attack, taken for granted and bored, are familiar aspects of her day. In trying to understand what kept her in this passive role for so long, she discovers many echoes from the past to do with home. She is shocked to realise how closely her life mirrors that of her mother, who also devoted herself to caring for home and family, instilling in Stella many 'workplace myths' about how this should be done. Stella also realises that she has copied her mother's passivity in accepting both her father's criticism, when transferred to her after her mother's death, and the criticism directed at her for many years by Jeff. She is now using the techniques recommended for the workplace, to assert herself further at home, thus improving conditions in what is also her working environment.

Andrew sometimes plays power games

At first Andrew is amused at the very idea of having to psyche himself up in order to challenge a colleague's behaviour. He cannot imagine himself meekly waiting for somebody in authority to acknowledge him. 'I'm not afraid of the boss – I am the boss!' is his initial reaction. Then he begins to wonder what it is like to be one of his employees. On the whole he feels he maintains a reasonable team spirit, but realises his feedback tends to be critical rather than positive. Ruefully he has to admit that his style of leadership is very like that of his secondary school headmaster. Sandra agrees, adding that a more supportive attitude would improve relationships at home as well as work.

Andrew also admits that he plays power games on site, deliberately keeping people waiting, or taking up more than one parking space or using his mobile phone in meetings. He realises this stems from a childhood myth that you have to be a top-dog in order to survive. Although he is committed to changing his attitude at work, he says he draws the line at negotiating win-win solutions in boxing and rugby matches!

GETTING THE MOST FROM THIS CHAPTER

1. Invent some colleagues whose behaviour sometimes enhances and sometimes disrupts the smooth running of the workplace. Role-play these characters with a friend, practising giving and receiving positive and negative feedback until you feel comfortable with both.

2. Choose a particular area of conflict in your workplace. Practise and then use the techniques described in this chapter to help resolve it.

3. Record your results and comments in a separate section of your journal devoted to asserting yourself at work.

6

Becoming Assertive in Everyday Life

In the last three chapters we looked at various 'kit-bags' of attitudes and behaviours we may have acquired to help us function in certain situations. Some would have been learned by imitation, some by observation, and some by direct instruction. In each case, an important part of the learning process was the feedback we received from others. Whether verbal or non-verbal, this feedback let us know which behaviours were acceptable and whether, in general, we were shaping up. If it was mainly positive, it would have helped us to develop a favourable view of ourselves. Frequent negative feedback would have had the opposite effect.

As we saw in Chapter 1, success, assertiveness and feeling good about yourself are interrelated. Success often depends more on valuing yourself and your abilities than it does on your actual talents. When you celebrate yourself (which is not the same as boasting) the world responds in kind. When feelings about yourself are negative, success may elude you. Our **self-concept** – the way we think and feel about ourselves – underpins our approach to every situation. How positive is yours?

LOOKING AT YOUR SELF-CONCEPT

How do you feel about yourself now? If you could express that feeling in one word, what would it be? If you were asked to think of five or six words which describe you, what would they be? Write these words in your progress journal.

Your choice of words may be related to feedback you have received about yourself over the years. Did you choose mostly positive or mostly negative words? Did 'assertive' and/or 'successful' appear on your list? Are you happy with the way you feel about yourself? Are there things you would like to change? Take some time to think about this.

Asking some important questions
Allow about an hour to complete this three-part exercise. Think very carefully about each question, then answer it as fully as you can. Write the answers in your progress journal.

1. How well do I know myself?

● Who am I?

● What do I want?

● Why am I here?

● Who do I love?

● Who loves me?

● What do I believe in?

● What do I look like? (Be very specific.)

● What am I good at?

● What is the most important thing in my life?

● Am I happy with myself?

When you have answered these questions as fully as possible, put the answers to one side and relax for a few moments before moving on to the next section.

2. Why do I do what I do?

● What are you wearing today? Take your mind back to the moment when you put on each item of clothing. What were your exact reasons for choosing it?

● What did you do yesterday? Take some time to recall each event in your day. What were your reasons for doing each of these things?

● What have you done so far today? How will you be spending the rest of the day? What are your reasons for doing those things?

How many of these things were done because you wanted to do them? Why did you want to do them? How many things did you do for other people? Why did you do them? How many things did you do because you had to? Why did you feel you had to? Which choices were made because of what other people might think or how they might see you? Did any particular person or persons come to mind? Take some time to think about your answers.

3. Whose life am I living?

● Are you happy with the amount of choice you feel you have in your life? Are you happy with the balance between things you do because you want to do them and things you feel obliged to do?

● Do you find yourself in situations where you feel disadvantaged, disempowered or manipulated? Are you unable to think of what to say or do until afterwards?

● Do you feel you are generally in the driver's seat? If not, who is – and what would you like to do about this?

● Are you happy with your life and the way you live it?

● Are there any changes you would like to make?

Before moving on to the next section, take some time to reflect on the answers you gave to the questions in the last three exercises.

WORKING ON YOUR SELF-CONCEPT

What did you discover about yourself and your self-concept in the last section? How might this view of yourself have been formed? What do you feel about the part other people's opinions of you may have played – or might still be playing – in this process?

The following three-part exercise is designed to help you trace past and present influences on your self-concept and turn them to your advantage. The first two sections are diagnostic. Allow about half-an-hour to complete them, then take a break before continuing with the activities in the third section.

1. Identifying outside influences

● Take a large sheet of paper and divide it into two columns. Head one Positive Messages and the other Negative Messages.

- Take some time to think about all the feedback you can remember receiving about yourself over the years, whether verbal or physical, favourable or otherwise. List each incident in the appropriate column. Include reactions to your character, personality, abilities, prospects, appearance – whatever comes to mind.

- Beside each one, note whether it was a 'one-off' reaction or a repeated message.

- Think of everyone from whom you might have received such messages: family, friends, neighbours, doctors, nurses, dentists, therapists, salespeople, teachers, other authority figures, those you work with and for, acquaintances, strangers. Beside each positive or negative message, note the person who conveyed it.

2. Assessing the effects

- Take some time to think about each incident you have noted. How did you feel when it happened? What are your feelings when you remember it now?

- How might each incident relate to the discoveries you made about yourself and your self-concept in the last exercise? Which messages fed your confidence and raised your self-esteem? Which had the opposite effect? Which still affect you now?

When you have worked your way through both lists, remember to take a break before starting the next section.

3. Making the changes you want

a) Working with words

- Go through your list of positive messages again, highlighting the ones which still boost your energy. File these in your memory for use when your self-esteem is low.

- Go through your list of negative messages, highlighting any which still affect you adversely. Re-run each of these incidents several times in your mind, imagining yourself defusing the negative feedback with the techniques suggested in Chapter 5 (agree with any truth in the statement or disagree if there is none, ask for clarification, respond assertively to any put-downs).

- Change the highlighted positive messages into 'I' statements (eg favourable reactions to your skills or appearance become: 'I made an excellent job of . . .' 'I look great in my mauve shirt,' etc). Repeat these statements aloud several times.

- Replace the highlighted negative messages with positive 'I' statements to the contrary. Repeat these positive statements aloud several times.

b) Positive visualisation

Read these instructions onto a tape, leaving suitable pauses for your response.

> Imagine yourself as you want to be – confident, healthy, successful, living the life you want . . . Imagine it in great detail . . . your appearance, expression, gestures, voice . . . See yourself living in the house you want . . . What is this house like?
>
> See yourself working . . . shopping . . . walking down the street . . . meeting friends . . . having fun . . . behaving and reacting as you would like to behave and react.
>
> See yourself having a great time at a party . . . Notice how other people react to you. Notice their expressions . . . their body language . . . things they say.
>
> Imagine yourself in many different situations, looking, behaving, and sounding happy and successful.

- Persevere with this visualisation until you begin to notice changes in your feelings and behaviour.

- Do all the exercises in this section every day for at least two weeks.

CHECKLIST

- Success, assertiveness and a positive self-concept are closely linked.

- Feedback from others has a significant effect on our developing self-concept.

● An important step in becoming assertive is to identify what we really believe and feel and need rather than following the dictates of others.

FOCUSING ON YOURSELF

Do you like to keep other people happy? Who keeps you happy? Take some time to think about this.

Many people feel uncomfortable with the idea that their own happiness is important, and tend to play down their needs for fear of being selfish. Identifying and meeting our own needs are assertive acts which, far from being selfish, release others from the responsibility of doing this for us.

As our sense of self-worth increases, we begin to feel more confident about claiming our space. We begin to realise that we are as important as our fellow beings, and that our needs matter as much as theirs. Once this is understood we can begin to make some rational decisions about how much time we wish to devote to others and how much to ourselves.

Identifying your needs

When choosing what to wear, what to do, what to eat, how often do you stop and ask yourself 'What do I really want?' Saying 'I don't mind' when faced with a choice can become a habit. Breaking that habit by paying attention to yourself and your needs may seem strange and difficult to do at first. If this is so for you, persevere.

● Focusing on yourself and your needs helps to develop a sense of self-worth.

Rest, relaxation and fun, are very important needs which frequently get marginalised. Many people feel anxious, even guilty, about taking a break from work. This is usually the result of old and unhelpful programming which should be erased (see Chapter 2).

● Organising sufficient quality leisure time for yourself is an assertive, self-affirming act.

Look again at your responses to section 2 and 3 in answering some important questions above. What reasons did you give for making your everyday decisions? How much choice did you feel you had? Are you happy with what you discovered? Do you feel you pay sufficient attention to yourself and your needs?

- What will you change as a result of asking yourself these questions?

RESISTING MANIPULATION

There are people whose anxiety levels rise when they are unable to control others. They will use a variety of manipulative tactics, subtle and otherwise, to get those around them to dress, eat, behave, even think, in certain ways.

Parents, teachers, managers, law enforcers and salespersons do this to some degree as part of their role. Outside such roles people may behave manipulatively either because they need others to fit their picture of how the world should be, or because they want something and are unable to ask for it assertively. Manipulators usually home in on our area of greatest insecurity. Whether their motives are personal or professional, we need to be aware of such tactics when they are being employed. We also need to have our repertoire of assertive responses ready to deal with them. Some common areas of insecurity are described below.

Appearance

Many of us can identify with the female comedian who constantly asks 'Does my bum look big in this?' Insecurities about the way we look have made fashion, slimming, health, beauty products and cosmetic surgery into multi-million dollar industries.

Faced with a barrage of persuasive sales tactics, including photographs cleverly doctored to show us how we 'ought' to look, it can be difficult to make choices that are wholly our own. The exercises about influence and feedback which you did earlier in this chapter will be very helpful in this respect, as will the habit of asking 'What do I *really* want?' as suggested in the previous section.

In matters of appearance, we are also likely to be influenced by the reactions and comments of those around us – perhaps more so than we realise. For example, is there a colour you 'wouldn't dream of wearing'? Think back. Has anyone ever said to you something like 'People with your colouring can't wear red', or 'Purple does nothing for you'? How about the old adage 'Blue and green should never be seen'? Has that ever influenced your choice of colour combination?

Take some time to think about this in relation to all aspects of the way you look – or the way you 'wouldn't dream of' looking. Positive or negative feedback about your appearance can be handled assertively by using the tactics described in Chapter 5 (handling criticism, and handling praise).

Dieting

This is an activity which can trigger some highly manipulative responses from people who seemingly cannot bear someone to exert more control than them. They assail the would-be dieter with comments such as 'A little bit more won't hurt you', 'Don't be silly – you know you want some', and 'Go on – spoil yourself'.

One way to avoid this is not to mention that you are dieting. Instead assertively state what you want and do not want to eat, without offering an explanation. If this does not work, or if the person concerned already knows you are dieting, asking for clarification is an excellent way of stopping the game. Say calmly, 'Why is it important to you that I eat that?' Another useful tactic is to practise saying 'no' and *meaning* it (see trying new techniques below). If your 'no' has subtle undertones of 'well I might if you just pushed hard enough', the person concerned will home in on this and push.

Cutting down/stopping drinking or smoking

The strategies involved in resisting opposition to your diet apply here also. Instead of saying that you are cutting down or giving up, say 'I don't drink', or 'I don't smoke'. If the person concerned knows you are cutting down or have stopped, and still insists on trying to persuade you to do otherwise, use a firm 'no' and/or the question 'Why do you want me to have a drink/cigarette?'

Spending

Many people would like us to give them money. Some put a lot of effort into trying to persuade us to do so. With friends and family, asking for time (see Chapter 4) and asking for clarification before making a decision are appropriate responses.

With unsolicited telephone and doorstep sales, it is best not to engage in any kind of dialogue. The person concerned will almost certainly have learned a technique for taking advantage of any response other than an unequivocal 'no thank you', followed by a replaced receiver or closed door. If your feeling is 'Poor thing – it's their job', disregard it. That is their problem, not yours.

Likewise, letters 'informing' you that you have won either £50,000 or a surprise gift are best not answered but consigned to the bin – which applies to all junk mail. That constant stream of invitations, special offers and 'helpful' suggestions is not poured through our letter-boxes in order to do us a favour. If there happens to be something there that you never thought of – it is because you never needed it!

TRYING NEW TECHNIQUES

Saying no

For most of us there are times when we find it very hard to say no. In which situations and with which people does this apply to you? What about dieting, having sex, resisting a hard sell, doing someone a favour, lending books? Take some time to think about this.

Being able to choose to say no at such times, thereby making life more comfortable for yourself, takes practice. Try the following steps:

1. Practise saying 'no' loudly and often when you are on your own.

2. Practise saying 'no' assertively with a partner. Ask for feedback on both your verbal and non-verbal behaviour when doing so.

3. Role-play one of your difficult 'no' situations with your partner and get feedback.

4. Practise saying 'no' in real situations. Do *not* practise the most difficult nos first – you will probably discourage yourself.

A phrase like 'I'm not happy with that can sometimes feel more comfortable than 'no'. You might like to start in this way.

Rehearsing for success

Like asking for time, rehearsing for success is a useful habit to cultivate. If we ask for something with the underlying expectation that we will not get it, or apply an assertiveness technique with the underlying feeling that it may not work, we are rehearsing for failure – and that is what we are likely to get. If instead we prepare ourselves for a situation in which we are going to succeed, we greatly increase our chances of doing so.

I have a right to be wrong

I have a right to speak

I have a right not to speak

I have a right to be listened to

I have a right to be me

I have the right not to be trivialised

I have the right to shut my door

I have the right to some free time

I have the right to choose what I do in my free time

I have the right to a lunch break

I have the right to proper nourishment

I have the right to be tired

I have the right to be disappointed and depressed

I have the right not to please everyone all of the time

I have the right to say no

I have the right to be consulted

I have the right to be kept in the picture

I have the right to forget

I have the right to change my mind

I have the right not to explain

I have the right not to feel guilty

Fig. 6. A sample bill of rights.

RELATING ASSERTIVELY TO OTHERS

Getting on with the neighbours

Just as the work environment can trigger memories of school, living among your neighbours can feel family-like and may mirror some of your experiences in your family of origin. If you were not accustomed to privacy, you may find your territory invaded by people coming into your house or garden, perhaps borrowing things and asking later. If you were a child who tended to get left out, you might find yourself not invited to neighbourhood events. You might find that people tend not to turn up to your parties – or that you are the one who usually gives the parties, and this may mirror the way things were in your childhood.

You might find that neighbours frequently talk to you about their troubles or ask you for help, which might be how it was for you as a youngster – and who do you go to?

If you do find history repeating itself in this way, you are probably giving off subtle signals that this is what you are used to and therefore how you expect life to be. As with rehearsing for success, you can change this by *expecting something different*.

The first step in changing your expectations is to be clear about your rights and needs.

Drawing up a bill of rights

● Make a list of the things that are important to you in terms of rights and needs.

● Turn this into your individual bill of rights (see Figure 6).

● Place this bill of rights where you can see it frequently. Repeat it aloud to yourself every day until you really believe it and can easily convey that belief to others.

Complaining with candour and charm

A problem which many people find calls for assertive behaviour, is that of noisy neighbours. Loud music is a common complaint. You can assertively ask for the volume to be turned down or for the music to be played at socially acceptable times. If a straightforward request is not successful, use three-stage message followed if necessary by recorded announcement – if possible with a smile.

Some things are more difficult to approach, for example family rows and noisy sex. Complaining about a noisy kitchen appliance attached to a party wall, or a dog that barks incessantly while its owners are out can seem petty, even though the noises in question drive you to distraction. Again three-stage message and recorded announcement can be very useful, particularly if preceded by rehearsing for success. If the subject feels embarrassing or petty, calmly express the dilemma:

● 'I feel uncomfortable saying this because it's rather embarrassing/sounds petty but . . .'

These guidelines also apply to complaining in other situations, eg when returning faulty or unsuitable goods to a shop. Always rehearse for success. Expect to be treated with charm and to get what you want, and this may happen. If not – get tough! In this situation recorded announcement comes into its own.

● 'These shoes have split and I would like a refund. Yes I know they were in the sale, but they have split and I would like a refund . . . Yes I understand it's not your policy to give refunds on sale goods, but they have split and I would like a refund . . . ' etc.

SKILLS PRACTICE

1. A neighbour who never returns borrowed items until asked several times wants to borrow your mower. They say they only need it for an hour. It always comes back caked in mud and you have to clean it before you can use it. What do you say?

2. Your next-door neighbours go on holiday leaving their teenaged son alone in the house. He has several parties and plays music very loudly until the early hours of the morning despite being asked repeatedly to turn it down. How do you attempt to resolve this at the time? What do you say to your neighbours on their return?

3. The meal you have ordered in a restaurant turns out to be very disappointing. The waiter asks 'Is everything all right?' What do you say?

4. A friend buys you an expensive item of clothing for your birthday. You discover a hole in it. What do you do?

CHECKLIST

We can increase our levels of assertiveness and self-worth by:

- identifying and meeting our own needs

- remembering to ask 'What do I really want?'

- learning to resist manipulation

- learning to say no and mean it

- rehearsing for success

- changing our expectations

- drawing up a bill of rights and honouring it.

CASE STUDIES

Howard and Andrew sort things out

Andrew has been storing equipment in Jenny and Howard's garage – an arrangement which was supposed to be temporary, but has now continued for several years. Jenny feels angry about this intrusion on their space and for some time has been asking Howard to get Andrew to move it. Howard has made a few half-hearted attempts, but Andrew always manages to manipulate him into letting the arrangement continue. Now Jenny has been promoted and will have to travel further to get to work so she and Howard need a second car. She wants Andrew's stuff moved before the new car is delivered and says she will tell him herself.

Howard feels he cannot let her do this in case Andrew becomes aggressive. He practises three-stage message and recorded announcement, and psyches himself up by rehearsing for success before calling on Andrew. Andrew says it will be very inconvenient for him to find another storage space, which is true. Howard calmly tells him this is not his problem, which surprises Andrew greatly, but he continues to try to wear Howard down. Using recorded announcement, Howard sticks to his guns. Andrew suddenly recognises the technique, and is about to make a sarcastic comment to that effect when he realises the courage it must have taken for Howard to confront him in this way. He also realises that it is his own aggressive behaviour which has had this effect on his mild-mannered neighbour. He apologises and negotiates a date for moving the stuff. However, old habits prompt him to push for extra time. Encouraged by his success so far, Howard calmly states that he will agree to Andrew's use of the garage for a further week only if Andrew pays rent for that week and also pays for Jenny's new car to be garaged nearby during that time. Andrew is impressed by Howard's new attitude and moves the stuff the next day.

Stella asks for a lift

Stella's family are beginning to recognise her as a person with a life that is separate from her various roles. She is finding it more difficult to change perceptions outside the home with people she sees less frequently. She is trying to focus more on her own needs and not do quite so much for other people, but friends and neighbours who still see her as capable, reliable and there for everybody, frequently call on her services.

With great difficulty at first, she starts asking neighbours to get shopping in for her and one day rings her friend Mary and asks her for a lift into town – something she has never done before. There is a stunned silence at first, and then Mary asks if she is ill. In her progress journal Stella records the incident as 'asked Mary if I could have a life' and thought this was an interesting Freudian slip. Eventually Stella finds she rather likes having things done for her, and when people ask for her help she begins to make bids for reciprocal arrangements.

GETTING THE MOST FROM THIS CHAPTER

1. Return to the section Looking at your Self-concept several times over the next few weeks. Refer to your notes and record any changes or new insights in your progress journal.

2. Think carefully about your wants and needs and anything which might be influencing these.

3. Practise the suggested techniques.

4. Say an easy no and a difficult one. Start a section in your journal specifically about saying no.

7

Handling Anger

Allow yourself to feel the anger and recognise that it is your power. Visualise a volcano going off inside you and filling you with power and energy.

Shakti Gawain: 'Living in the Light'

Like fire, anger is a good servant but a bad master. If suppressed, it can eat away at you inside or burst out destructively in unexpected places. If given free rein it may overwhelm and frighten you and those around you. If properly processed and honestly expressed, it can become the basis of assertive action.

LOOKING AT YOUR OWN ANGER

In order to be able to use our anger purposefully, we need to form a relationship with it. We need to know what triggers it, how it affects us, how we tend to react and how this might need to be changed.

Knowing what pushes your buttons

- When was the last time you were really angry? What were the circumstances? Who were you angry with? What did you do and say?

- Make a list of all the times you can remember being angry during the last two years. Make a note of what happened, who was involved and how you reacted. When you have finished, note any patterns which may have emerged.

- Who or what made you the most angry you have ever been in your whole life? How did you react then?

- Take a fresh sheet of paper. Begin 'What really makes me angry is . . .' Write for five minutes without stopping.

- Take another sheet of paper. Begin 'I get really angry with people who . . .' Write for five minutes without stopping.

What have you learned about yourself through doing this exercise?

Understanding your physical reactions

Generally speaking, we get angry because we feel under attack – either personally, or in relation to our opinions about the world and how it should function. Anger is a response to fear. In our primitive state it would have been necessary to enable us to defend ourselves, our families, our territory and possessions. The physiological changes which take place when we are angry, therefore, have a primitive life-preserving function. To some degree (depending on how controlled we are) we grit our teeth, clench and maybe brandish our fists, narrow our eyes to see the 'enemy' more clearly, and tense our bodies for the 'attack'. Our mouths may become dry as energy is re-routed from the digestive system to other parts of the body which are more crucial to the **fight-or-flight response**.

Clearly, the resources which our bio-chemical system makes available to us at such moments are meant to be used. If as a 'civilised' person we habitually suppress anger, its effects may turn inwards, producing physical symptoms such as tension headaches, back pain and digestive disorders. Suppressed anger is also likely to surface unexpectedly and vent itself in a totally unrelated situation – the **kicking the cat** syndrome.

● Which of these 'primitive' responses do you find yourself making when you are angry? What do you tend to do with these responses?

Working on your emotional reactions

● What do you feel about the statement 'Anger is a response to fear'?

● How do you cope with fear?

● How do you cope with anger?

● How were these emotions handled and expressed in your family of origin?

● How did the adults react when you expressed these emotions?

● What effect did this have on you?

● Do these childhood experiences influence the way you handle these emotions now?

● Are there any changes you would like to make?

Dealing with your anger and fear

1. Establish exactly which of these emotions you are feeling (or which is dominant).

2. Admit it fully to yourself, and allow yourself to *feel* it. Often, acknowledging 'I am afraid' or 'I am angry' rather than trying to deny it to yourself can release any power that the emotion has over you.

3. If appropriate and possible, express the emotion verbally or physically. If you are in a situation where it would be inappropriate to express your feelings *choose control*, but honour your feelings by promising to process them later – and do so.

4. If your feelings are to do with another person, tell them and clear the air. (Three-stage message might prove helpful here.)

5. Use the energy generated by your anger or fear to bring about positive change.

CHECKLIST

Anger:

- is a response to fear

- may prompt similar coping strategies to the ones we developed in childhood

- triggers a series of physical reactions designed to help us defend ourselves

- can be overwhelming and frightening when these reactions are not understood

- can be contained by acknowledging and expressing it

- can become the basis of assertive action when these processes are understood.

ENCOUNTERING ANOTHER PERSON'S ANGER

In the previous section, you looked at the way anger was handled and expressed in your family of origin, and at what effect that might have had on you. The way you react to someone else's anger now may also be connected with these experiences.

Looking at your reactions to other people's anger

Do angry people frighten you? Do you react by becoming angry too – or do you feel anxious and intimidated? Does your reaction depend on what form the other person's display of anger takes?

Which of these angry behaviours have you experienced?:

- shouting

- swearing

- sarcasm

- threatening behaviour

- physical violence

- damage to property

- a barrage of words

- silence

- emotional blackmail

- indifference

- walking out

- inaction when action is desperately needed (**passive aggression**).

Which have you found most difficult to cope with? How did you feel when they were happening? What did you do? Which did you experience as a child? How did you feel and react then? Is there any connection?

DEALING WITH THE LEFTOVERS

- Choose a time when you were confronted with one of the behaviours you identified above. Try to remember exactly what the other person said and how they behaved.

- Imagine yourself responding assertively, using some of the techniques you have learned (eg asking for clarification, or selective agreement if the angry display was verbal, or three-stage message if non-verbal).

- Repeat your response aloud, if possible to a partner who will give you feedback.

- Repeat the whole exercise several times, choosing other incidents to work with.

If you encounter any of these behaviours in future, how do you think you might feel and react?

RESPONDING ASSERTIVELY TO AGGRESSIVE BEHAVIOUR

It is helpful to remember that an angry person is often a frightened person too. It is also helpful to remember that you are not responsible for the other person's feelings – nor can you cope with those feelings. You can only cope with your own.

Prepare yourself for making an assertive response, by memorising and practising the following routine:

1. **Breathe evenly** (a very important first step) and ask yourself:

   a) What is that person trying to convey?
   b) What am I feeling?

2. **Separate** the two and process your feelings (as in steps 1 and 2 of dealing with your anger and fear above). With practice, these preliminaries take only a few seconds.

3. If the person's aggression is verbal:

   - **Acknowledge** their anger.
   - **Ask** for clarification.
   - **Empathise** and express a wish to try to find a solution.

4. If the person continues to behave aggressively, try and get them to **lower their voice** and, if possible, **sit down**.

5. If this does not work:

●   **Level** with them. Explain politely but firmly any adverse effect that their behaviour is having on you. Say what you will or will not be able to do to help.

If the aggression is non-verbal, use three-stage message, followed if necessary by step 5 above. Remember to expect a favourable outcome; rehearse for success.

CHECKLIST

We can learn to respond assertively to other people's anger by:

●   knowing which behaviours we find it difficult to cope with

●   working through our earlier negative experiences

●   remembering that angry people are often frightened

●   separating the angry behaviour from our reactions to it, and working with the latter

●   breathing evenly

●   learning some appropriate techniques

●   rehearsing for success.

CASE STUDIES

Howard's parents kept their anger hidden

Howard rarely heard his parents raise their voices. If he did something which made his mother cross, she would tell him she felt 'sad', although her expression would be distant and detached. His father sometimes described things as 'exasperating', but said this in a very mild voice. For years Howard presumed that his parents did not get angry. As a result he felt ashamed of his own angry feelings and tried to pretend he did not have them. When he thought about his mother's frequent migraines and his father's stomach ulcer, he began to wonder whether his parents has been doing the same. Lately Howard has been suffering from headaches, and has also been told by his dentist that he grinds his teeth. As a result he has decided to make a conscious effort to express what he is feeling. At first he finds it difficult to identify exactly which emotion he is experiencing – unhappiness and anger frequently become confused.

After his confrontation with Andrew about the garage, he suddenly realises he is feeling angry. Eventually he is able to express this, first to himself then – after a few practices – to Jenny. She is delighted that he is starting to share his feelings with her, and he says he feels much 'lighter' as a result of doing so.

Stella confronts her father's anger

It is some months since Stella successfully challenged her father's aggressive behaviour. He has not shouted or thumped the arm of his chair since, but lately he has started subjecting her to long spells of angry silence, which she finds much harder to cope with. She wonders why it makes her feel so anxious, and them remembers that this was how her father showed his disapproval of her when she was little. Often she would not know what she had done wrong and would beg him to tell her, but he would refuse to answer. Now she has realised that her reaction to his silences is an echo from the past, she feels that next time she will be able to respond assertively. She has worked out an appropriate three-stage message and practised it with her older son, who thinks the whole thing is hilarious but has given her some helpful feedback on her body language. She is now waiting for an opportunity to make use of this message, and is busily rehearsing for success.

Andrew is afraid of being afraid

Andrew's reaction to the statement 'Anger is a response to fear' is derisory. He says he spent a great deal of his life being angry with people, but is not afraid of anything. Sandra asks him how he knows that, and what he thinks fear feels like. After thinking for a while he realises with something of a shock that being afraid is a terrifying prospect.

He says 'If I was afraid they'd make mincemeat of me.' When Sandra asks 'Who are they?' he starts to talk about his contemporaries in the neighbourhood where he grew up. He quickly recognises his 'fear of fear' is an echo from the past, and that he has been 'keeping himself angry' in order to overcome it. When Sandra suggests that fear could be a very useful emotion sometimes, he decides to try to do some work on getting in touch with it. He is surprised at how anxious this makes him feel.

SKILLS PRACTICE

1. Practise the routine for responding assertively to aggressive behaviour. Role-play your response with a partner.

2. Use the routine to respond assertively to someone who is aggressive in reality.

3. Practise all the techniques you have learned so far. Use each of them at least once in the coming week. Record the results in your progress journal.

4. When did you last say no and mean it? Make a note about this in your progress journal. Say no at least once today!

8

Taking Charge of Verbal Exchanges

In earlier chapters we looked at how past experiences can influence the way we behave, feel, think and generally present ourselves in the world. This chapter explores such influences further, using models from the **psychotherapeutic** approach **Transactional Analysis (TA)** developed in the late 1950s by Eric Berne. These models are in no way presented as 'the truth', but are simply aids to understanding some very complex processes. Because they are designed to be quickly understood and applied, they are useful aids to assertive communication.

Fundamental to the TA approach is Berne's **ego-state model,** also known as the **PAC model** because it depicts three basic aspects of our personality from which we can function: our Parent, our Adult and our Child (references to these are capitalised to distinguish them from parent, adult, child *per se*). All three can manifest at any age.

ASSESSING YOUR EGO-STATE

The ability to identify which of our ego-states is operating at any given time is a useful skill to cultivate. With practice, we can learn to make choices about whether we stay with the state or switch to another which would serve the situation better. The qualities of each state are described as follows;

Parent
In this state we behave, feel and think as our parents or as parent-figures might have done. The result may be **nurturing** (offering comfort, encouragement and support) or **controlling** (setting clear boundaries). The negative aspects of these Parent states are over-protection and repression.

Adult
In this state we behave, feel and think in a centred way, using our resources appropriately in response to the current situation.

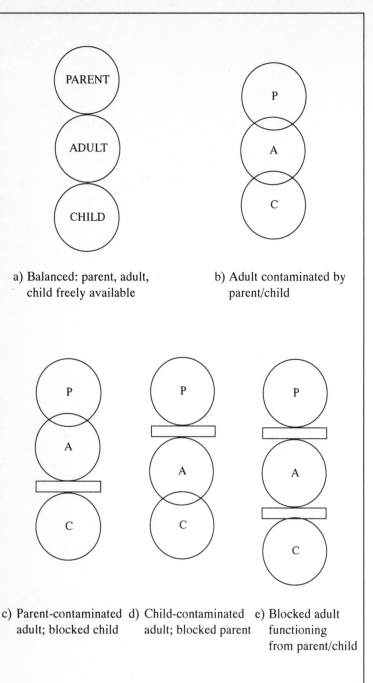

a) Balanced: parent, adult, child freely available

b) Adult contaminated by parent/child

c) Parent-contaminated adult; blocked child

d) Child-contaminated adult; blocked parent

e) Blocked adult functioning from parent/child

Fig. 7. Ego-states.

Child
In this state we behave, feel and think as we did in childhood. Our Child may be **free** or **adapted**. Our free Child wants to relax and have fun. Unchecked the fun could escalate into antisocial behaviour. Our Adapted Child helps us to keep such impulses under control, but can also intervene inappropriately and inhibit our ability to enjoy ourselves.

Understanding the Parent, Adult, Child model
The **PAC** model is an interdependent system rather than a hierarchy. Adult is always placed in the middle of the model because balance is achieved when we function from our Adult, with Parent and Child freely available to us (See Figure 7a). This is also the position from which we can be most assertive. Some less assertive positions are shown in Figure 7 as follows.

Figure 7b
This represents a situation where someone believes they are functioning from their Adult, when in fact they are strongly influenced by Parent/Child conditioning. An example of inner dialogue might be:

Parent:	Pink is such a vulgar colour.
Child:	I really like that pink shirt, but I wouldn't want to look vulgar.
Adult:	I've decided – pink is definitely not my colour.

Figure 7c
This represents an Adult with strong Parent overtones which block out both the needs and the contributions of the Child. Workaholics fit this model. A workaholic's script might be:

Parent:	You don't get anything in this life unless you work for it.
Adult:	I want to be successful, therefore I must work hard.
Child:	I'm tired. I want a nap. I want some fun.
Adult:	I'm too busy to stop at the moment.

Figure 7d
Represents an Adult with a seductive or intrusive Child which blocks out the voice of the Parent. People with addictions fit this model. In such a case an inner dialogue might run along the lines of:

Adult:	Being overweight is bad for my health. I must diet.
Child:	That chocolate cake looks really good.
Parent:	Show some self control.
Adult:	I'm an adult, I can decide for myself – and I think I deserve it!

Figure 7e

This represents a situation where the Parent/Child interaction absorbs so much energy that the Adult becomes unavailable. People whose behaviour and feelings fluctuate between extremes (eg people with certain types of eating disorder) fit this model. In the dialogue above, for example, the Parent/Child interaction might have continued ad infinitum, leaving the Adult beached and helpless. If Child managed to get the upper hand a binge might ensue. If Parent took over, a period of strict dieting or punitive vomiting might ensue. In extreme cases the person concerned might switch repeatedly from one to the other, with serious consequences for their health.

Finding what is predominant

Although all the ego-states depicted in Figure 7 may be experienced to some degree at various times, our family patterning will probably cause one to be predominant.

● What family patterns do you think might be associated with each of these ego-states?

● Which ego-state would you say is predominant for you?

● How does this affect your life in general?

● How does it affect the way you relate to others?

Exercise

1. Think back over the past 24 hours. Make a note of some situations when you were mainly in your Adult ego-state, some when you were in your Parent and some in your Child.

2. Take some time to recall each of these situations in detail. Exactly how were you behaving, thinking and feeling in each case? What were you saying inside your head? What was your body-language saying? Make some notes.

3. Do you notice any patterns of behaviour connected with these ego-states? How do you know when your Parent or Child has taken over? How will you use this knowledge in future?

CHECKLIST

Transactional Analysis:

● is based on a model of three interrelated ego-states: Parent, Adult and Child

● is an aid to understanding our behaviour, thoughts and feelings

● can help us to identify and carry out any changes which might be needed

● can help us to communicate more assertively.

MAINTAINING ADULT TO ADULT COMMUNICATION

To communicate assertively we need to be functioning from our Adult, with Parent and Child freely available (Figure 7a). When all persons concerned in the transaction are in this state, assertive Adult to Adult communication is achieved.

Understanding complementary exchanges

Figure 8a shows the **complementary exchanges** which can take place when two people are functioning from their Adult. Under these circumstances complementary shifts of ego-state can take place with the knowledge and agreement of both parties. For example, two friendly co-workers having lunch together might shift states as follows.

A1>A2: What time is it?
A2>A1: Five to two.
P1>P2: This is highly irresponsible! We ought to be getting back to the office.
P2>P1: Quite right. We've indulged ourselves quite enough for one day.
C1>C2: I haven't. Let's play hookey!
C2>C1: OK – we could say your car broke down.
A1>A2: I'm sorely tempted – but I guess we'd only have to make the time up later.
A2>A1: Yes – we wouldn't really gain anything – but it was a great idea!

Provided the response is as expected and the lines of communication are kept open, the exchange is complementary, but not necessarily

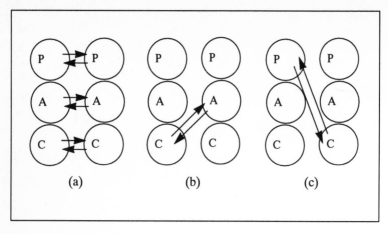

Fig. 8. Complementary exchanges.

assertive. P>P and C>C exchanges, where those concerned are not functioning from their Adult, can result in a slanging match. For example the previous conversation might have gone like this.

P1: I told you to watch the time. Now we shall be late.
P2: There you go – shifting the blame as usual!
P2: Keep your voice down. You're making a scene.
C1: So what – it's your fault.
C2: Oh – shut up! (Exits, leaving 1 to pay the bill).

In Figures 8b and 8c some other examples of non-assertive complementary exchanges are shown. A complementary C>A exchange, as in 7b, might occur when one person is thrown into their Child by a strong emotion, and appeals to another person's available Adult, as in:

C>A: I'm so angry I could kick somebody!
A>C: I can see how angry you are. Who is it you want to kick?

A complementary P>C exchange as in 8c might occur between an irate boss (Controlling Parent) and a mortified office worker (Adapted Child) who has made an error. A very different complementary P>C exchange might occur between a couple when one partner notices that the other is looking tired and offers a back-rub (Nurturing Parent) and the other responds enthusiastically 'Yes please – that would be great!' (Free Child).

Staying with your Adult

When you are functioning from your Adult and the other person involved is tending to do otherwise, there are a number of things you can do to help keep the exchange on an Adult to Adult basis.

1. Ask questions that will open out the discussion.

- What else can you tell me about this?

- What other angle is there?

- What kind of reaction have you had?

2. Ask for clarification.

- Could you explain that point again?

- Exactly who was responsible?

- Is this what you mean?

3. Check out the facts.

- Are those the correct figures?

- What is the source of your information?

- What date was this issued?

4. Acknowledge and empathise with the other person's feelings.

- I can see this has upset you.

- You're obviously concerned, and I can understand why.

- You've put a lot into this and you seem to be feeling undervalued.

5. Listen actively.

- Signal your attention with your body language.

- Show sympathy in your facial expression.

- Allow pauses for thinking and re-phrasing.

6. **Admit mistakes openly.**

● You're quite right – I made an error here in the second column.

● I know I was wrong about the timing of that.

● It was delivered to the wrong customer – my mistake entirely.

7. **Leave the door to negotiation open.**

● Perhaps there's another option.

● Perhaps we could look at that next time.

● Let's think about a new approach.

8. **Become familiar with your own ego-states, and use them from your Adult.**

● I'd like to sleep on this before making a decision (A).

● I can understand your impatience and I wish I could help (P).

● I need to relax now – fancy a game of squash? (C).

Disentangling crossed lines

Figure 9 shows some of the miscommunications which can occur when one ego-state is addressed and another one responds. In TA this is known as a **Crossed transaction**. For example, in 9a one person has communicated Adult to Adult. The other person has responded Parent to Child. Their conversation might have been:

$A>A$: What's for dinner?
$P>C$: Dinner – when you've been pigging crisps in front of the tele all afternoon?

In 7b an Adult to Adult communication gets a Child to Parent response, as in:

$A>A$: Did you phone airline about our reservations?
$C>P$: It's not fair. You expect me to do everything.

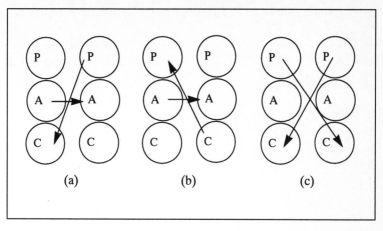

Fig. 9. Crossed exchanges.

In 7c person 1 uses their Parent to communicate with person 2's Child. Person 2 replies instead with their own Parent. The result might be:

P>C: Wrap up warm now. You know the wind's bad for your chest.
P>C: For heaven's sake! Can't you find something important to worry about?

A crossed transaction can usually be recognised by the feeling of bewilderment that ensues because the response has come from a totally unexpected angle – rather like a wrong number telephone call.

A suitably assertive counter-response would be selective agreement followed by recorded announcement. For example:

P>C: Dinner – when you've been pigging crisps in front of the tele all afternoon?
A>A: I may have eaten a lot of crisps, but I'd still like to know what's for dinner.

P>C: For heaven's sake! Can't you find something important to worry about?
A>A: Your health is important to me. Please think about wearing something warm.

LOOKING BELOW THE SURFACE

Surface exchanges sometimes cover **hidden messages**, which may be of a manipulative nature. Such messages are barriers to assertiveness, and we need to be aware of them.

Recognising hidden agendas

In Figure 10a and 10b, for example, the surface communication is Adult to Adult and the hidden messages are Child to Child, Parent to Child respectively. Examples would be:

A>A: That film you were talking about is coming to town next week.
Hidden C>C message: Can we see it together – go on ask me, please . . .
Hidden P>C message: It looks pretty rubbishy, but I expect you'll want to go anyway.

In Figure 10c the communication is Child to Child, with a hidden Parent to Child message. For example:

C>C: Let's go and see this new film – you'll love it!
Hidden P>C message: I'll show you what a good movie should be like.

A hidden message can be very difficult to detect. Even the person concerned may not be wholly aware of it. Because such messages are

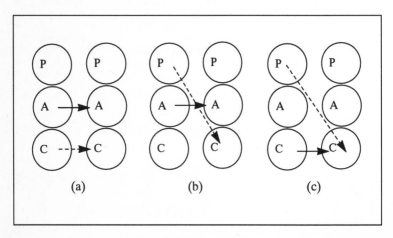

Fig. 10. Hidden messages.

secretive and often manipulative, they are barriers to assertiveness. In order to maintain clear Adult to Adult communication, we need to become aware of our own hidden agendas and either express them or do some work on them. For example, if the person concerned became aware of the last P>C message above, they might ask themselves, 'Why is this person's taste in films so important to me?'

● How would you express or process the hidden messages shown above?

● What hidden agendas might your recent communications have had? Would it have been helpful to express them? If so, how would you have done this?

Decoding double messages

Double messages arise from inner conflict, and are therefore contradictory. They are similar to hidden messages but more tricky, in that the person concerned makes a seemingly Adult to Adult statement while meaning the opposite. This shifts the original conflict, and the responsibility for resolving it, onto the recipient who is then in a double bind; 'damned of they do and damned if they don't' respond to the surface statement. Both parties may be unaware of the process.

Examples
In the examples which follow, the unspoken double messages appear in brackets.

1. 'I want you to tell Mum we won't be spending Christmas with her.' (If you do, I'll be mad at you for upsetting her.)

2. 'I want to do something to help.' (I want you to like my offer, but manage by yourself.)

3. 'Feel free to call at any time.' (I shall be relieved if you don't call at all. If you do, pick a time that suits me.)

4. 'I just want you to be yourself.' (Provided that conforms to my expectations.)

The only way to deal with such messages assertively is to bring them into the open. If you suspect you are on the receiving end of a double message, say something like, 'I get the feeling you are not sure about this', or 'Could you be more specific?'

If you catch yourself about to deliver a double message, identify the dilemma involved and express it. In the examples given above the people concerned might say:

1. 'I want us to spend Christmas by ourselves this year, but I don't want to hurt Mum. How shall we deal with this?'

2. 'I'd like to offer to help, but I'm really busy at the moment,' or – possibly nearer the truth – 'I feel guilty not offering to help, but I really can't face it at the moment.'

3. 'I'd like to say call any time, but I know that doesn't always work out. Is there a time when I can call you?'

4. This is a non-starter. Wanting someone else to be a certain way is a non-assertive attitude which requires processing.

Dispensing with scripts

The TA idea of a **life-script** is like a verbal version of the family kit-bag described in earlier chapters. It is based on childhood messages, duly absorbed and translated into a survival plan which we may continue to follow unconsciously as an adult. When we respond from our life-script we are running on other people's programs from the past, so our responses cannot be assertive.

Life-script material may be identified by statements which begin, 'I always . . .' 'I never . . .' 'It isn't right to . . .' 'I should . . .' 'I ought . . .'. It may reveal itself in views you have never questioned, recurring patterns in your life, your approach to life in general, your hopes, your fears and your expectations of how life will be.

● Take some time to think about each of these things then, with as little thought as possible, jot down some personal statement beginning 'I always . . .' 'I never . . .' etc. Make notes about any patterns or attitudes you discovered.

● With the help of these notes, record your current life-script in your journal. Reflect on it for a while.

● How does this script affect the way you are living your life at present?

● How would you like this to change?

● Think of times when you have been caught up in your life-script. How did it feel? What were you saying/doing? Recall your body language and facial expression. What were you saying to yourself? Write the answers in your journal.

Assertive Adult to Adult communication requires scripts to be discarded so that each person can respond authentically to the situation.

The verbal and non-verbal clues you noted in your journal will help in this respect, by alerting you to any switches into scripted behaviour – which in turn may be part of one of the counter-productive behaviour sequences which Berne described as **games**.

Identifying Games
Games are not funny. They are defences to protect people from greater or lesser degrees of pain.
                              Thomas A. Harris: I'm OK – You're OK

In observing human interaction, Eric Berne noted a number of predictable patterns and outcomes which he classified as games. To qualify as a game, the behaviour sequence in question must fulfil these criteria:

● There is a clearly identifiable set of rules (see example below).

● The underlying motives are different from what is being played out on the surface.

● The players play without adult awareness, going through each replay without realising they are doing it, unaware of having set the game up for themselves.

● For the main players there is a well concealed but definite pay-off.

In his book *Games People Play*, Berne sets out the rules of many games and gives them names, such as: *Now I've Got You, Son of a Bitch, Look How Hard I Tried,* and *Why Don't You? Yes But.* He describes the rules of the latter as follows:

> One player who is 'it' presents a problem. The others start to present solutions, each beginning with 'Why don't you . . .?' To each of these, the one who is 'it' objects with a 'Yes but . . .' A good player can stand off the group indefinitely until they all give up, whereupon 'it' wins.

The pay-off in this case might be the confirmation of a firmly held belief, eg nobody can help me, plus the removal of any pressure to change the situation.

Games usually end with everyone feeling confused, misunderstood and wanting to blame each other. They often serve to reinforce the player's life-script, so that people seek out others whose games interlock with their own. Since assertive Adult to Adult communication cannot take place when games are being played, it is essential that we learn to identify our games, understand our need to play them, and eventually let them go.

What games do you play?

- What keeps happening to you over and over again?

- How does it start?

- What happens next? And then?

- How does it end?

- How do you feel?

- How do you think the other person feels?

- What hidden message might you be giving them when you play this game?

- What hidden message might the other person be giving you?

Make a note of your answers in your journal. Do you notice any connection between your games and your life-script? How will you use this information to help you move forward?

CHECKLIST

In TA terms, the following are barriers to Adult to Adult communication:

- non-Adult complementary exchanges

- crossed transactions

- hidden agendas

- double messages

- scripts

- games.

N.B. This chapter has offered only a brief introduction to a very thorough and rewarding method of studying human behaviour. For further information on TA, please see Useful Addresses and Further Reading.

CASE STUDIES

Howard and Jenny stop playing games

Howard realises that for many years he played I'm Only Trying to Help You and What Would You Do Without Me? in his relationship with Jenny. This has fed Jenny's feelings of inadequacy and kept her in a helpless role. His pay-off was feeling needed and loved. Jenny realises she has played Stupid and Poor Me in response, her pay-off being the comfort she got from Howard's fatherly behaviour. She also realises that she has angrily played Husbands Are Stupid and If It Weren't For You I Could . . . before she was finally able to summon enough assertive energy to start functioning from her Adult. Howard knows that unresolved issues from his childhood sometimes cause him to play Wooden Leg (What do you expect from a guy with a . . .) and Ain't It Awful. He feels Jenny is leaving him behind in this respect – until she confesses to having played Let's You and Him Fight to manoeuvre him into confronting Andrew, whom she dislikes.

She readily admits that her pay-off was a wonderful feeling of Now I've Got You, Son of a Bitch when Andrew moved his stuff out of their garage. Howard and Jenny have found this a useful way of identifying unproductive patterns in their relationship. Working on these together is helping them both to behave more authentically.

Stella sorts out some double messages and hidden agendas

Stella is enjoying her changing role within the family. Having made time for herself, she has enrolled in a yoga class and a counselling course. Jeff teases her about both, until their younger son tells him to give it a rest. Stella is grateful, until he reveals his hidden agenda by asking her for some money. Jeff tells Stella he was 'only kidding' and that of course he supports her 'one hundred per cent'. However, after a few evenings of heating up meals she has left, and twice having to iron his own shirt, he begins to complain. Stella realises that his 'one hundred per cent' for her venture is conditional on her attending to his needs first. She feels very disheartened and decides she should at least give up the yoga class to keep the family happy. Then she realises she is falling into an old pattern of compromising her needs in order to keep the peace.

She confronts her husband and son with their unsupportive behaviour – which they both deny – and assertively states that she will take whatever time she needs to complete the counselling course to her satisfaction.

Andrew gets rid of his script

Andrew knows he has a life-script which says 'Families stick together. Outsiders are trouble. Never let them see you're scared. Hit first and ask afterwards.' He realises he put this together as a young child with childish perceptions, emotions and responses.

Although it helped him to survive some tricky situations at the time, it does not serve him now. Recently he has begun to understand this and has started trying to change his behaviour. Sandra has helped him to recall some of the situations from his childhood, paying particular attention to how his script operated at the time. Her feedback about his body language and facial expression, together with his own observations about his feelings and inner dialogue, have helped him to identify exactly what takes place when he switches into scripted behaviour. These clues are enabling him to recognise the process early on and change to a more assertive Adult mode.

SKILLS PRACTICE

1. Clean up your act! Use the work you have done in this chapter to help you eliminate crossed lines, hidden agendas, double messages, scripts and games.

2. Resolve to replace these non-assertive responses with clear Adult to Adult communication.

3. Work at it.

4. Record the results in your journal.

9
Assessing Your Progress

It is recommended that you re-read Chapters 1-8, then put the book aside for at least two weeks and practise before completing the exercises in this chapter.

If you have worked your way through this book, completing the exercises, practising the techniques and keeping your journal up to date, you will have noticed a number of changes by this stage. Take some time to think about this.

● What changes have you noticed in the way you feel about yourself?

● What changes have you noticed in your attitude to other people?

● What changes have you noticed in your behaviour?

● When did you first notice these changes taking place?

● What affect have they had on your everyday life? How do you feel about this?

● Make some notes in your progress journal.

COMPARING YOUR RESULTS

Reassessing your assertiveness
When you started working with this book, you completed an assertiveness self-assessment (Figure 1). Complete it again now, without looking at your previous scores. When you have done this, compare the two.

● Which items got a higher score this time?

● Was this what you hoped for or expected?

● Were any of your scores lower this time? If so, why do you think this was?

● Which results are you particularly pleased with? Why?

● Which items do you feel need further work? What will you do about this?

Turn back to the section Defining your Terms. What does the word 'assertiveness' mean to you now?

Make each of the definitions in this section into an 'I' statement: 'I am able to ask clearly for what I want or need', 'I have the confidence to say what I am feeling', 'I have clear personal boundaries' etc. Make these 'I' statements aloud, taking time to notice which you feel particularly confident in saying and which may need further work. Make a note of the latter in your progress journal.

● How do you feel about your progress after doing these exercises?

● On a scale of 1-10, how assertive would you say you are now?

Reconsidering your self-concept
Turn back to Chapter 6.

1. Read the first paragraph of the section entitled Looking at Your Self-Concept. Answer the questions in your progress journal, *using your non-dominant hand*. (Writing with our non-dominant hand can put us in a more vulnerable, child-like state of mind, which makes us less likely to censor what we write. In this case, concentration on the physical difficulty involved also helps to distract you from remembering what you wrote last time.) Compare your answers to the ones you gave the first time you did this exercise.

● What difference do you notice?

● Were your answers more assertive or less assertive this time?

● Why do you think this might be?

2. Move on to the three-part exercise Asking Some Important Questions. As before, allow about an hour to complete it. Read your answers through and reflect on them before comparing them with the ones you gave last time.

● What difference do you notice?

● Is this what you would have expected?

● How positive is your self-concept now? Mark yourself on a scale of 1-10.

If you feel you need to, re-read your notes from the three-part exercise Working on Your Self-Concept which follows the section you have just completed. It might also be helpful to repeat the positive 'I' statements you made in 3a. Do this several times, looking at yourself in a mirror as you speak.

3. Read through the section Focusing on Yourself, answering the questions mentally. Make a note of any changes in your attitude since last time. How good are you now at paying attention to yourself and your needs? Mark yourself on a scale of 1-10.

REVIEWING YOUR JOURNAL

Take some time to read through the notes you made for each chapter. Make a note of your thoughts and feelings as you read, particularly where you notice any changes. Use the following guidelines to help you.

Chapter 1

● Check out any changes in your use of body language, voice and facial expression (especially your eyebrows!) How do these changes feel?

● Did you find working with a role model helpful? In what way?

● What further work do you need to do in this respect?

Chapter 2

● Was it helpful to you to identify earlier role models and understand how you might have copied them unconsciously? Did you find the role-play in Exercises 1 and 2 helpful? What further work might be needed?

● What effects have Rewriting the Family History and Changing the

Energies of Your Inner Family had on your feelings about yourself? How do you expect this to affect your life?

- What did you learn about yourself in relation to your school days? Did Re-empowering Your Inner Child help to change your feelings about yourself? What effect has this had on your life so far?

- How have you got on with using Asking for Clarification and Three-Stage Message?

Chapters 3 and 4

- What did you learn about family roles and family communication in both your past and your current family situation?

- Re-read your notes from the long visualisation exercise Staging a Family Discussion (Chapter 3). What are your thoughts and feelings about this now?

- What did you learn about your 'family kit-bag'? Were you able to compare kit-bags with your partner? What did you find out?

- How has what you learned from these exercises helped with any current difficulties? What has changed? What further work needs to be done?

- Have Expressing the Dilemma, Owning the Feelings, and Selective Agreement helped you to communicate more assertively with your family? Note any specific occasions when they have been useful. Which other techniques have helped in this respect? When have you used them?

- How are you doing with regard to being yourself in your relation-ships? On a scale of 1-10 how would you rate yourself in this respect?

- What score would you give yourself for assertive parenting? What changes have you made in this respect? Have Recorded Announcement and Asking for Time been useful?

- What have been the knock-on effects of the changes you have made? How are you managing these? Which techniques have you found useful in this respect?

Chapter 5

- What changes have you noticed in your levels of assertiveness in the workplace?

- What do you think about possible links between the workplace and school?

- Which Workplace Myths were familiar? Which have you worked on successfully?

- Which techniques have you found helpful in tackling workplace situations?

- Did you find yourself dealing with opposition and power games? How did you tackle them? What work remains to be done in this respect?

- On a scale of 1-10, how would you rate your skills in Giving and Receiving Feedback? How does this score compare with the one you would have given yourself before starting this book? What further work needs to be done?

Chapter 6

- What answers did you give to the questions on Resisting Manipulation? Which topics were of particular relevance to you? Were you able to use the suggested techniques to help you handle manipulation in these areas? How did it go? Do you need more practice?

- How are you getting on with saying no? How do you feel when you say it? What about Rehearsing for Success – has this been helpful?

- Do you believe your Bill of Rights yet? Have you had an opportunity to stand up for those rights by Complaining with Candour and Charm? How did that go?

Chapter 7

- Have you been angry lately? If so, what was it about? Was it the sort of thing that usually pushes your buttons? How did you handle it this time?

● Have there been any changes in your patterns of anger since doing this work? Are you angry more often/less often? Do you feel OK about expressing your anger?

● Have you noticed any changes in the way you feel when other people are angry? Which techniques have been most helpful to you in dealing with this?

● Read any notes you have made about anger in your journal. Do you notice any changes taking place? What further work needs to be done?

Chapter 8

● What do you think about TA as an approach? Have you found it helpful? Which aspects in particular?

● How have you worked with the TA models in this book? Have you used them actively, bringing the ideas and the language into your day-to-day communication – or have they been more useful as aids to understanding?

● Has the work you did in Chapter 8 helped you to communicate more assertively? On a scale of 1-10, rate yourself as an assertive communicator.

MAKING PLANS

In working through these chapters you have explored in some depth your mode of functioning in a variety of settings and situations, and you have begun to make changes where needed. Which results have pleased you? Which are you less happy with?

In reviewing your journal, which areas did you identify as needed further work? Make a list in order of priority, and draw up a work-plan. It is probably advisable to tackle one specific area at a time. How long will you spend on each topic? Which will you start with?

Decide how you would like to work on each one. Look back at the various approaches used in this book – eg affirmations, visualisation, working with a partner, TA. Which worked best for you?

Make a practice plan for each topic. Make a note of:

● **What** you want to achieve

● **How** you will work

- **When** you will work and for **how long**

- **Who** else will be involved.

Include regular practice of at least one specific technique in each of your plans.

CHECKLIST

You can maximise your progress by regularly monitoring:

- your non-verbal behaviour signals

- your assertiveness levels

- your skills

- your ability to stay in your Adult

- your level of self-esteem

- the feedback you receive from others

- the efficiency of your work-plan.

And remember – when practising any new skill, one of the most important qualities to cultivate is **perseverance**.

CASE STUDIES

Howard finds he has a more positive self-concept

Howard is pleased with the effects his assertiveness work has had on his relationship with Jenny, but feels rather despondent about his individual progress. Despite his success in confronting Andrew, he still feels quite unsure of himself after discovering the games that were being played in his life. Jenny reminds him that these were defences, which will become redundant as he grows more confident. He finds this reassuring. In the notes he made about his self-concept, he finds he originally described himself as 'Quiet, shy, hard-working, anxious, middle-aged.' He had not felt he was 'in the driver's seat', and frequently felt manipulated and disempowered. This time, with his left hand he has written 'Contented, humorous, shy, loving, courageous.' He realises he is beginning to feel more in control of his life and better able to stand his ground. He is surprised and pleased by these results.

Stella's assertiveness levels have risen

When Stella first did the Assertiveness Self-Assessment, she gave herself zero for the first three statements, and scores below five for each of the rest. When she assesses herself again, none of her scores is below six, and she gives herself two tens – for 'I have the confidence to ask for time to think things over' and 'I have clear personal boundaries and can state them.' When she checks the first notes she made about her non-verbal behaviour signals, she finds most of her characteristics listed under 'Passive'. This time she finds she has eliminated most of these passive behaviour signals and replaced them with assertive ones. She is delighted by these dramatic changes but not surprised, because she feels so much more confident, and is seeing the results of this in her life. With her new-found assertiveness, she feels she deserves her success after working so hard to achieve it.

Andrew feels he has taken a step backwards

Andrew's scores are much lower on the Assertiveness Self-Assessment the second time round, because the first time he gave himself ten for everything! He feels he has taken a step backwards instead of progressing. Sandra reminds him how scornful his attitude was towards most of the statements the first time. He had 'no problem' about standing up to aggressive people, or stating the adverse affect somebody's behaviour was having on him. He had laughed at the thought of feeling guilty about saying 'no' and so on.

He admits this was aggression rather than assertiveness, and that the high scores were allocated in a sarcastic way. After he and Sandra discuss this, they both feel that the fact he has thought about the statements properly this time, and marked himself quite low on some of them, represents a huge improvement in his attitude.

SKILLS PRACTICE

1. Plan your work carefully.

2. Practise the techniques regularly.

3. Persevere.

10

Using Your Skills

There is freedom from and freedom to, and now maybe you feel free to put your total energy into the work and make a destiny for yourself in this world.

Prem Deepak 'The Outer Worlds'

Assertiveness can open the door to new possibilities in every area of your life. As your assertiveness increases, you will experience:

- greater confidence in yourself

- greater confidence in others

- improved family relationships

- improved working relationships

- increased self-responsibility

- increased self-control

- decreased stress levels

- savings in time and energy.

Which of these have you experienced so far? What other benefits are you aware of? What would you like to achieve now?

To assist you further in developing and using your skills, this final chapter provides a series of easy-reference guides to key behaviours, attitudes and techniques. A partner's feedback might prove helpful in deciding which aspects need further work.

TARGETING KEY AREAS

Checking your body language
Eye contact
Look whoever you are addressing directly in the eyes. This is self-

assertive, and also lets the other person know they have your full attention. Not meeting their eyes can give away your power, detract from
your message, or make you appear disinterested.

Facial expression
Show your emotions when appropriate. Be genuine, eg do not smile
when you are angry or sad. Keep your eyebrows relaxed and level.

Posture
Stand tall with both feet firmly on the ground. **Sit** in a relaxed and open
manner, not crossing your arms over your body or winding one leg
around the other. Avoid hugging yourself, which makes you look and
feel insecure. Also avoid slumping, which makes you look dejected or
lacking in energy.

Gestures
Keep to a minimum – in most situations stillness is more effective. No
fist-shaking, arm-waving, finger-pointing or door-slamming. No 'ward-
ing off' gestures.

Proximity
Keep a reasonable distance (this varies from culture to culture). Do not
invade the other person's space by stepping or leaning into it. If somebody invades yours, step back and turn slightly so that you are at an
angle to them. If this does not work, tell them you feel uncomfortable
when they stand that close to you.

Distracting body language
No hair-twisting, foot-tapping, scratching, fiddling with fingers, looking
at watch, etc.

Checking your verbal behaviour

Use of voice

- Volume: Keep reasonably loud, not aggressively so – nor submis-
  sively quiet.

- Tone: Keep firm and natural, not putting on a wheedling, submissive
  or childish voice.

- Speed: Keep moderate. Fast talking can indicate that you are nervous.

● Inflection: Monitor carefully for hints of sarcasm, aggression, defensiveness or put-down.

Choice of words

Use	Avoid
Clear, brief 'I' statements: 'I feel' 'I'd prefer' 'I disagree'	Rambling, generalised statements. Using 'You' 'We' 'They' 'One' instead of 'I'. Asking 'Don't you prefer?' 'Wouldn't you rather?' instead of stating your position. Padding: 'Well' 'Like' 'You know.' Justification: 'I shouldn't really say this but . . .' Self-effacement: 'I hope you don't mind' 'I'm sorry to bother you but . . .'
Suggestions without 'shoulds' and 'oughts': 'How would you feel about . . .' 'Maybe we could . . .'	Heavy handed advice: 'You ought to' 'You really must . . .' Threats.
Constructive criticism: 'That might work better if you . . .' 'Have you considered . . .' 'I find this works for me.'	Using destructive criticism (ie criticising without making constructive suggestions). Being sarcastic. Using put-downs.
Owning of feelings: 'I get irritated when you interrupt me.' 'When you shout, I feel frightened.'	De-personalised or generalised statements: 'It's annoying.' 'People get on my nerves.' Blaming.
Invitation to comment: 'What are your feelings on this?' 'How would you tackle it?'	Pushing your own views forward. Presenting your views as 'the way'. 'Do it like this.'
Acknowledgement of choice and responsibility: 'I choose to/not to . . .' 'I am not prepared to make that effort.' 'I allow people to take advantage of me.' 'I don't need this, I'm buying it because I want it.'	Saying 'I can't' 'I must' 'I have to' rather than taking responsibility for your choices. Blaming circumstances. Confusion between wants and needs.

Assertiveness means:

Valuing myself, who I am and what I do.

Taking responsibility for myself, my thoughts, my actions and my feelings.

Recognising my own wants and needs as separate from those of others.

Making clear 'I' statements about my thoughts and feelings.

Saying 'I choose to' rather than 'I have to.'

Allowing myself to make mistakes.

Allowing myself to enjoy my successes.

Feeling comfortable with criticism or praise.

Allowing myself to change my mind.

Asking for what I need.

Asking for time to think things over.

Setting clear boundaries.

Saying 'no' without guilt.

Being confident enough to speak out.

Being confident enough to remain silent.

Being responsible *towards* others – not *for* them (unless they are children).

Respecting other people and their right to be assertive.

Being able to state the adverse effect somebody's behaviour is having on me.

Being able to stand up to aggressive people.

Being able to deal with most situations comfortably.

Fig. 11. Assertiveness checklist.

| Distinction between fact and opinion:
 'That is how I see it.'
 'My experience is different.' | Making generalised statements:
 'Everyone knows' 'It's obvious'
 'Of course'. Presenting your <br> views as facts. |

MONITORING YOUR PROGRESS

Read through the Assertiveness Checklist (Figure 11) turing each definition into an 'I' statement:

● How many of these statements can you now make with confidence?

● Which statements need further work?

● How do these results compare with previous assertiveness self-assessments?

● What action will you take?

REVIEWING THE TECHNIQUES

For easy reference, the ten techniques you have learned are listed below, together with their uses.

1. Asking for clarification
When somebody's remark or request takes you by surprise, calmly ask them to explain what they mean.

● 'What is it about my idea that you find ridiculous?'

● 'Exactly what is it about my behaviour that upsets you?'

Use when:

● you need time to think

● somebody is being critical

● somebody is letting off steam at your expense.

2. The three-stage message

a) **Identify the behaviour** which you find unacceptable. Be very specific.

b) **State the effect** this behaviour has on you. Again, be very specific.

c) **Ask for the change** you would like.

Use when:

● you wish to negotiate a specific change in somebody's behaviour – particularly if you find them unco-operative or intimidating.

3. The five-stage message

This is a more detailed and formal version of the three-stage message. The steps are:

1. **Identify** the other person's problem behaviour.

2. **State** the tangible effect this behaviour has on you.

3. **Say** how you feel about that.

4. **Ask** for the behaviour change you want.

5. **Invite** the other person to comment.

Use when:

● a formal situation, such as a work setting, requires delivery of complicated or precise feedback.

Getting a three-stage and five-stage message across

● If the other person raises a distracting side issue, **acknowledge** it without being deflected from your purpose. Say something like: 'We can talk about that as soon as we settle this.'

● If the other person does not seem to be hearing or understanding, ask them to **repeat** what you have said. Say something like: 'What do you think I am asking you to do?'

4. Expressing the dilemma

When you are not sure how to approach someone, or how to tackle a situation which concerns them, express the dilemma to them and invite their help in solving the problem.

Use when:

● you find yourself engaged in an inner dialogue about somebody.

5. Owning the feelings

Basically, this means taking responsibility for your own feelings and not blaming them on a person or a situation. Instead of saying 'You make me/it makes me feel', say 'When you do this/when this happens, I feel . . .'

Use:

● whenever you are discussing how you feel.

6. Selective agreement

When somebody criticises you, agree with any truth you can find in their statement.

● 'Yes, I am untidy sometimes.'

● 'You're right. I might regret not taking an umbrella.'

If you can find no truth in the statement, say 'I don't see it that way' or 'We obviously have different views. What can we do about that?'

Use when:

● somebody's remarks might otherwise push your buttons.

7. Recorded announcement

1. **State** your case in as few words as possible.

2. **Listen** to what the other person has to say and acknowledge it.

3. **Repeat** your original statement in the same words – like a recorded announcement.

Use:

● for getting your point across in the face of strong opposition.

8. Asking for time
A useful habit to cultivate. Say: 'I need to think about that' and then set a time for giving your decision.

Use when:
● a suggestion or request is sprung on you suddenly.

9. Saying no
Practise the following routine for learning to say no without feelings of guilt:

1. Say 'no' loudly and often when you are on your own.

2. Say 'no' assertively to a partner. Ask for feedback on both your verbal and non-verbal behaviour when doing so.

3. Role-play one of your difficult 'no' situations with your partner and get feedback.

4. Say 'no' in real situations. Do *not* say the most difficult nos first – you will probably discourage yourself.

5. A phrase like 'I'm not happy with that' can sometimes feel more comfortable than 'no'. You might like to start in this way.

10. Rehearsing for success
Like Asking for Time, this is a useful habit to cultivate. Whatever you undertake, prepare yourself for a situation in which you are going to succeed. This greatly increases your chances of doing so.

CASE STUDIES

Howard gets feedback on his body language
Howard notices that when people talk to him they often become irritable and make excuses to cut the encounter short. He thinks they must find him boring which is a blow to his self-esteem. When he discusses this with Jenny she decides to observe his behaviour at a drinks party. She

notices a tendency to tap his foot, drum his fingers on his folded arms and glance surreptitiously at his watch. She recognises these as signs of shyness and discomfort, but realises that someone who does not know Howard might interpret them as boredom. She also notices his difficulty in maintaining eye-contact, and wonders whether his glancing around the room might also seem like lack of interest in what is being said. Finally she notes that throughout the evening his eyebrows are raised in what she knows to be an expression of anxiety, but which makes him look rather arrogant.

Howard finds her feedback very useful, as he had been totally unaware of these mannerisms and the impression they might be creating. He decides to concentrate in changing one aspect at a time, starting with his facial expression. He is now finding that keeping his eyebrows level is in itself helping him to feel confident, so that the other mannerisms are tending to subside.

Stella feels good about saying no

Despite all her hard work and her success in other areas, Stella is feeling increasingly guilty about cutting down on the help she gives to relatives and neighbours. She finds herself returning to the old pattern of agreeing automatically to their requests, particularly on the phone when she is unprepared for them. In resolving to deal with this, she finds the grouping together of three items on the assertiveness checklist very useful. She feels confident with the first two – Asking for Time to Think Things Over and Setting Clear Boundaries. This encourages her to tackle the next item, Saying No Without Guilt – a goal still to be achieved. She copies these out and places them beside the phone to remind her of her purpose. She then follows the recommended practice routine for learning to say no, and combines this with Rehearsing for Success (see items 9 and 10 above). After a somewhat shaky beginning, she begins to find the routine fun, and persuades her younger son to practise it with her. The most difficult nos, which she saves until she feels reasonably confident, are to her father and his sisters. After she has said them, she feels really good about affirming her personal boundaries in this way.

Andrew practises some techniques

Andrew has never had any difficulty in getting his point across, so he does not feel the need to learn techniques such as Three- and Five-stage Message, Asking for Time and Recorded Announcement. However, on seeing Expressing the Dilemma, Owning the Feelings and Selective Agreement placed together as items 4, 5 and 6 of the review list, he realises he has difficulty with all of them.

With Sandra's helps he has begun to practise them, and has already found Expressing the Dilemma a very useful alternative to winding himself up with an internal dialogue. He finds Owning the Feelings more difficult, but always feels good when he has managed to do it. Selective Agreement, however, goes completely against the grain and he can hardly force himself to say the words. He says they 'stick in my throat'. Sandra finds this hilarious and is encouraging him to 'loosen up' in this respect. His children shriek with laughter when he manages to say things like 'I may not be the tidiest person in the world', and he is beginning to see the funny side of it himself. He feels that being able to laugh at himself in this way is a sign that his confidence is growing.

GETTING THE MOST FROM THIS BOOK

1. Follow up the suggestions for further reading which interest you most.

2. Continue to practise and monitor your progress, using the easy-reference guides in Chapter 10.

3. Ask your friends for feed-back.

4. Keep your progress journal up-to-date.

5. Re-read the book and repeat the exercises in three months' time.

Glossary

Active listening. Using body language, facial expression and vocal encouragement to indicate that the speaker has your full attention and interest.

Affirmation. Positive auto-suggestion using an inspirational phrase.

Aggression. A hostile defensive reaction.

Body language, non-verbal behaviour. Conscious or unconscious communication via posture, gesture, breathing and facial expression.

Buttons, triggers. Events which provoke habitual emotional or behavioural responses.

Complementary exchange. (TA) A communication where the ego-state which is addressed is also the one which responds.

Coping strategies, defences, survival mechanisms. Habitual responses which have proved helpful in the past but may not be appropriate to the current situation.

Crossed transaction. (TA) A miscommunication in which one ego-state is addressed and a different one responds.

Denial. Conscious or unconscious refusal to acknowledge the facts of a situation.

Double message. A statement, the underlying meaning of which is contradictory.

Ego-state model, PAC model. (TA) Eric Berne's representation of three basic areas of the personality from which an individual can function: Parent, Adult and Child.

Emotional blackmail. Controlling another person by manipulating their emotions.

Empathy. The ability to put yourself in someone else's shoes.

Family dynamics. The way in which a family functions.

Family patterning, conditioning. Attitudes and behaviour learned in the family of origin.

Feedback. Messages from various sources about ourselves and our behaviour.

Fight-or-flight response. The physiological changes triggered by the adrenalin system in response to threat.

Free/Adapted Child. (TA) Aspects of the Child ego-state.

Freudian slip. An unconscious word-substitution which reveals a hidden thought.

Game. (TA) A term used by Eric Berne to describe an identifiable sequence of behaviours with a predictable outcome.

Hidden agenda. An unrevealed motive behind a statement or request.

Inner child. The part of ourselves that thinks, feels and reacts as we did in childhood.

Kicking the cat. Venting anger inappropriately.

Nurturing/Controlling Parent. (TA) Aspects of the Parent ego-state.

Passive aggression. Showing hostility by doing nothing.

Passive/submissive behaviour. Giving control to someone else or to the situation.

Personal boundaries. The limits set by an individual on what they are prepared to do and allow.

Power game, power move. Action or sequence of actions by which one person seeks to control another.

Projection. Unconsciously transferring the characteristics of one person or situation onto another, and reacting to the latter accordingly.

Psychotherapeutic. Having to do with psychotherapy. Psychologically healing.

Reinventing. Creating anew. This psychological intervention works on the premise that life is largely a 'story we tell ourselves', so we may as well tell ourselves a better one.

Role model. A person whose behaviour we consciously or unconsciously copy.

Script, life-script. (TA) A survival plan worked out in childhood, which still operates in adulthood.

Self-esteem, self-worth. The extent to which we value ourselves.

Self-concept, self-image. Our overall view of ourselves.

Significant adult. A person who had a considerable influence on us during our formative years.

Transactional Analysis (TA). A psychotherapeutic approach first developed by Eric Berne in the late 50s.

Win-win solution. A negotiated solution where there are no losers.

References and Further Reading

EMOTIONAL AND PHYSICAL HEALTH

Achieving Personal Well-Being, James Chalmers (How To Books).
The Healing Power of Illness, Thorwald Dethlefson and Rudige Delke (Element).
You Can Heal Your Life, Louise Hay (Eden Grove).

PERSONAL AUTONOMY

Building Self-Esteem, William Stewart (How To Books).
Choosing Not Losing, Dorothy Rowe (Fontana).
Creating Self Esteem, Lynda Field (Element).
Gestalt Self Therapy, Muriel Schiffman, (Wingbow).
Living in the Light, Shakti Gawain (Nataraj).
Mind Power, Dr Vernon Coleman (Century).
Self Counselling, William Stewart (How To Books).
Staying Ahead, John Wareham (Thorsons).
Take Charge of Your Life, Louis Proto (Thorsons).
The Power is Within You, Louise Hay (Thorsons).
The Successful Self, Dorothy Rowe (Fontana).
Unlocking Your Potential, Peter Marshall (How To Books).

RELATING ASSERTIVELY

Peoplemaking, Virginia Satir (Souvenir Press).
The Dance of Intimacy, Harriet Goldhor Lerner (Thorsons).
The Relate Guide to Better Relationships, Sarah Litvinoff (Vermillion).

TRANSACTIONAL ANALYSIS (TA)

Born to Win, Muriel James & Dorothy Jongeward (Addison Wesley).
Games People Play, Eric Berne (Grove, Penguin and others).
I'm OK – You're OK, Thomas Harris (Pan and others).
TA Today, Ian Stewart & Vann Joines (Lifespace).

VISUALISATION WORK

Creative Visualisation, Shakti Gawain (New World Library).
Life Choices and Life Changes Through Imagework, Diana Glouberman (Unwin).
Reclaim Your Power, Kaleghl Quinn (Mandala).
Walking Through Walls, Will Parfitt (Element Books).
What We May Be, Piero Ferrucci (Turnstone Press).

Useful Addresses

BUSINESS AND PROFESSIONAL ISSUES

Carole Spiers Associates, Gordon House, 83-85 Gordon Avenue, Stanmore, Middx. HA7 3QR.
Navigator, 79 Dean Street, London W1V 6HY.

FAMILY AND RELATIONSHIP

Parent Network, 44-46 Caversham Road, London NW5 2DS.
Relate: local branch information in phone book.

COUNSELLING

British Association for Counselling, 1 Regent Place, Rugby, CV21 2PJ.

KNOWING YOUR RIGHTS

Citizens' Advice Bureau: local branch information in phone book.

PERSONAL GROWTH PRODUCTS AND INFORMATION

Lifetools, Freepost SK 1852, Macclesfield SK10 2YE.
New World Music Ltd, Freepost ANG 441, The Barn, Beccles, Suffolk NR34 8BR.
Rontronics, 96 Dartmouth Park Hill, London N19 5HU.

TRANSACTIONAL ANALYSIS (TA)

ITAA, 1772 Valejo Street, San Francisco, California 94123, USA.
EATA, Case Grand-Pre 59, 1211 Geneva 16, Switzerland.
British Institute of Transactional Analysis, BM Box 4104, London WC1 3XX.

Index